"If you're a new Christian and wc [...] reading this book? My friend Aa[...] [...] what it's like to be an adult convert to Christianity. He writes with simplicity, transparency, humor, and humility, outlining essential wisdom for this stage of the journey. I can't think of a better book to give a new follower of Jesus. After the Bible, it's the best book for new adult Christians that I know of."

ERIC SCHUMACHER,
pastor; podcast host; author of multiple books, including *Ours: Biblical Comfort for Men Grieving Miscarriage,* and *Jesus & Gender: Living as Sisters and Brothers in Christ* (with Elyse Fitzpatrick)

"I can relate to Aaron's story. While I am now in full-time Christian ministry, I was not raised in a Christian home. I resonate with the humor and candor in this book, and so appreciate the simplicity of how Aaron elaborates on our new life in Christ. He dives deep, but in a way that is readable and accessible to all. This book will be a welcome and helpful companion to any new adult follower of Jesus."

JEN OSHMAN,
author; women's ministry director

"I find it surprisingly hard to find a book to give to new Christians. Some assume too much; others sound preachy. That's why I'm glad to read *I'm a Christian—Now What?* It's honest, clear, scriptural, and relatable. Not only that, but it deals with issues often ignored by other books. I can't wait to share it with people in my church."

DARRYL DASH,
pastor, Liberty Grace Church, Toronto, Ontario; author of *8 Habits for Growth*

"This book is easy-to-understand—and yet nowhere dumbed-down—counsel that will help new Christians answer their questions and to figure out what questions to ask next."

RUSSELL MOORE,
editor-in-chief, *Christianity Today*

"I can't begin to tell you how many times I have wanted to reach for a book like this to pass along to a new believer and struggled to find one that was both biblically grounded and accessible. Armstrong has given us a helpful resource here, and I look forward to putting it into the hands of as many new Christians as I can. And if you are one of those new Christians reading this endorsement, read on friend. Here is a useful guide for you."

RUSS RAMSEY,
pastor; author of *Rembrandt is in the Wind: Learning to Love Art through the Eyes of Faith*

"I've long been on the hunt for a book to give a new believer without completely overwhelming them. *I'm a Christian—Now What?* is the book I will gladly recommend and hand out liberally. Aaron Armstrong tackles the questions new Christians will ask in an engaging and accessible way that will remind them again and again what a joy it is to follow Jesus."

GLENNA MARSHALL,
author of *The Promise Is His Presence*
and *Everyday Faithfulness*

"Aaron Armstrong's story of encountering Christ and then growing as a Christian is full of ups and downs, and more than a few surprises. *I'm a Christian—Now What?* combines personal stories and wise principles that will aid the person who has just come to faith and wonders what the road ahead should look like. Aaron's insight and guidance will make this a go-to book for new believers."

TREVIN WAX,
vice president of research and resource development at the North American Mission Board; visiting professor at Cedarville University; author of *The Thrill of Orthodoxy*, *Rethink Your Self*, and *This Is Our Time*

"As a pastor, I've always struggled with the question of what resource to first put in the hands of a new convert. We want to guide a new Christian on their journey but we don't want to overwhelm them, to push them into the deep end of the pool before they are ready to swim. This is why I am grateful for this important resource. Writing from the perspective of someone who was there not long ago, Aaron Armstrong is the perfect guide for a new believer. With simplicity, clarity, and biblical precision, *I'm a Christian—Now What?* is the book every pastor should have at the ready. Every church should buy these in bulk. And every Christian should have a stack of them in their home. To fulfill the Great Commission, we must make disciples and this resource is a helpful, vital tool in the hands of God's people."

DANIEL DARLING,
director of the Land Center for Cultural Engagement; bestselling author of several books including *The Dignity Revolution*, *The Original Jesus*, *The Characters of Christmas*, and *The Characters of Easter*

"Aaron has written both wise and practical words that speak well to the questions and insecurities that new believers experience. Pastors and churches should consider this a valuable first step toward discipling recent converts."

RONNIE MARTIN,
lead pastor of Substance Church;
author of *The God Who Is With Us*

"Aaron has written something here that is immensely helpful and practical. In all reality, most 'mature' Christians should read this book too—to remind ourselves of the basics of why we do what we do, and to remember how to love those who are new believers among us. This book feels like a true friend coming alongside another friend who is learning how to find their way in this new life. It's solid and true, kind, gentle, and easy to read and apply. Certainly one to share over and over again."

ANDREA BURKE,
writer; podcast host; director of women's ministry,
Grace Road Church, Rochester, New York

"Aaron Armstrong is friendly and thoughtful, which makes him exactly the sort of person who should help a new believer take his or her first steps. Here he has written an accessible book that I would gladly give to a new believer in my church or community."

CHRIS MARTIN,
author of *Terms of Service*

"There are few resources today that are both substantive and easy to read, which is all the more important when writing to new Christians about how to live. Thankfully Aaron does both, providing new Christians with a path to journey into the Christian life in a way that is full of grace and practicality. As a pastor, I can't wait to walk through this book with the new adult Christian's in my church and help them grow into all that Jesus has made them to be."

JEREMY WRITEBOL,
lead campus pastor, Woodside Bible Church, Plymouth, MI;
author of *Pastor, Jesus Is Enough*

"Aaron has a sharp mind for discipleship coupled with a pastoral heart for people and the result is a helpful resource for those new to the Christian faith—those the Scripture says have been 'born again.' When someone is born physically, loving parents and doctors wrap the child in care as the child has entered a whole new world. In the same way, when we meet Jesus we enter a new world—a new kingdom—and we need to be supported and nourished with grace and truth. I am thankful for this book, as it does just that."

ERIC GEIGER,
senior pastor, Mariners Church, Irvine, CA

"With wit and wisdom, care and candor, Aaron has provided a practical resource for walking with God. This book is filled with simple steps to grow in your faith, foundational truths of Christianity, and helpful stories from Aaron's own conversion to Christianity. *I'm a Christian— Now What?* is bound to encourage you as you move forward in your relationship with Jesus."

KATIE ORR,
author of *Secrets of the Happy Soul*
and the FOCUSed15 Bible Study series

I'M A CHRISTIAN—

NOW WHAT?

**A GUIDE TO YOUR NEW
LIFE WITH CHRIST**

I'M A CHRISTIAN—

NOW WHAT?

A GUIDE TO YOUR NEW LIFE WITH CHRIST

AARON ARMSTRONG

LEXHAM PRESS

I'm a Christian—Now What?: A Guide to Your New Life with Christ

Lexham Press, 1313 Commercial St., Bellingham, WA 98225
LexhamPress.com

Print ISBN 9781683596714
Digital ISBN 9781683596721
Library of Congress Control Number 2022942974

Lexham Editorial: Elliot Ritzema, Claire Brubaker, Katrina Smith, Mandi Newell
Cover Design: Brittany Schrock
Typesetting: ProjectLuz.com

*For Adam, who obeyed even though he
was pretty sure God was wrong.*

CONTENTS

FOREWORD

This is the book I wish someone had handed to me years ago when I sat curled up alone in the fetal position on the floor of my tiny dorm room, blinking through tears, far from home yet closer to Home than I had ever been before. I had just welcomed Christ into my heart—Oh joy! Oh relief! And yet ... Oh *my* ... what a slow but steadily building trepidation I felt. Suddenly everything rolled together: the realization of what living this meaningful life would now actually mean. How messy! None of my family were believers. Very few of my friends. I was engaged to an atheist. I was a Shelley scholar, for goodness' sake. And—*alas!*—an *academic*.

My rejoicing hallelujahs soon took on the minor tones of dread.

All this new Jesus stuff was just, well, so *complicated*.

And overwhelming.

And alienating.

How to be in the world and not of it? I mean, *really*? The Bible ends with "Lord Jesus, come." There is no postscript that tells you how to break up with your unbelieving partner, until he does.

How do we get up off the floor, from wherever we have been flung and undone and made new by grace, and walk through the door that has been opened before us? Just how do we step into Oz, into Narnia, into this new Jerusalem disguised as our still very ordinary home or workplace or hangout, but now filled with gawkers or worse—those who do not see at all?

This is the book I wish I had to orient myself when I left the City of Man for the City of God. For when I had to navigate the roadblocks, potholes, and roundabouts along the way.

Yes, this is the book I wish had kept stashed in my pocket when I realized that being a follower of Jesus Christ came with joy and excitement and a clarity that made everything technicolor, while it also came with some big, fat, personal—as well as cultural—inconveniences.

Whether you are being pulled from the slough of despondency by a fellow pilgrim or you are trading good for best in an earnest self-examen, once you have become a Christian—indeed—*now what?*

With self-effacing courage, Aaron Armstrong answers this question and the other questions lurking behind it. When it comes to taking the leap of faith, many of us find ourselves still in midair. Armstrong's gracious storytelling, however, provides a soft landing. His narrative style allows us to put both feet firmly on the solid ground secured for us in Christ.

I was delighted this book finally found my hands, my eyes, my heart, and my spirit. Admittedly, it is difficult not to hold an affinity with an author who hails from my own hometown, who has also had an adult conversion to Christianity, who has also married way up, and who has also—*get this!*—relocated as a Canadian to the Nashville area. But what really makes us kindred spirits is our kinship in Christ. I appreciate how Armstrong reveals that kinship with each of his readers through deep and discerning compassion, relatability, and vulnerable care. He looks at our equally toppled apple carts, surveys the mess, and then helps us pick up the fruits of our scattered spirits and realign them with living our best lives, now and evermore.

This book is deceivingly effective. While we are nodding in agreement, seeing ourselves in the awkward moments, and quite often laughing our heads off, Armstrong is deftly and dedicatedly leading us through the post-conversion labyrinth by untangling all the threads in which we have ensnared ourselves: the puppet strings of an anti-faith culture; the weeds of worry, lethargy, or despair; the mind-forged manacles of our own sin and doubt. With winsome wisdom, Armstrong helps us understand what it is to order our loves truly and righteously, and thereby to live richly in this reordering as a blessing to ourselves, to others, and to our Lord.

This always-timely book is seriously funny and amusingly profound! With searing honesty leading to hard-won wisdom, Armstrong has penned a must-read for all seekers of the meaning of life, and even *more* of a must-read for those who discover this meaning and seek to earnestly live by it. There is a strange and powerful relief in this little narrative handbook that only the truth can bring. In his whimsical yet sobering storytelling, Armstrong reminds us of the often countercultural yet necessary alignment of our values with the relentless reality of joy.

Dr. Carolyn Weber
New College Franklin
Franklin, TN
August 2022

WHAT IS LIFE

//

MAKING SENSE OF LIFE WHEN
EVERYTHING IS THE SAME—EXCEPT YOU

Imagine waking up one morning and being you, but *not*. You get out of bed and look in the mirror. *What's different?* you wonder. You still look like you—you haven't magically switched bodies with your best friend or your teenage self. No new gray hairs as far as you can tell. A six-pack didn't appear overnight. You lean in as close as you can to the mirror, so close that you're about to leave a mark. Still, there's nothing different. You're the same *you* as you were before you woke up this morning.

Back in the bedroom, your unmade bed is where you left it, with the same sheets and blankets you slept in the night before. The same clothes you've always worn hang in your closet. The same pile of laundry—the one you've been meaning to get to for the last week—languishes in the corner of the room. You get dressed in clothes that fit the way they always have. You grab your usual breakfast, which tastes the same as always. You take the same car on the same route and get to work at the same time you always do. Your workday is the same: the same tasks, meetings, and coworkers. Everything seems the same, but you can't shake this feeling that something has changed. And something has. Even though everything is the same as it ever was, *you* have changed. *You* are different.

You're still the same you, but you are not the same you that you were before.

You're not imagining it. This is really happening. It began the moment you became a Christian. Whether it was a few days, weeks, or months ago, something happened to make you realize you needed to believe in Jesus—a man who is also God, born a little over two thousand years ago without the involvement of a human father, who performed miracles, taught people what it meant to live as people who love God, offended just about every religious leader he came into contact with, loved people his society rejected, was crucified, and rose from the dead on the third day following his burial (1 Corinthians 15:3–4).[1]

Now what? What does it mean to be the same person, but *not*? What does this mean for your life, your relationships, your job, your *everything*?

The short answer is that it means *everything* to your everything. But to get why that's true, let's make sure you understand what exactly happened when you believed in Jesus and why you're now in this you-but-not-you situation.

1. The earliest debates in the church were about the nature of Jesus, how he could both be God and human, because the Bible shows him to be both. Since around the time of the Council of Chalcedon (a gathering of church leaders and theologians in AD 451), Christians have described Jesus as being fully human and fully divine, one person within whom there are two natures "without mixture, change, division, or separation."

SO WHAT HAPPENED TO YOU, ANYWAY?

If you believe in Jesus, you are a Christian. But what exactly does that mean—and how does believing in Jesus change everything about your whole life? Here is the quickest way to understand it:

When you believe in Jesus, you become a new person.

In John 3, Jesus speaks with a man named Nicodemus, a well-respected Jewish leader, a teacher very familiar with the part of our Bibles we call the Old Testament. Nicodemus goes to see Jesus to find out what his deal is. He and the other religious leaders know Jesus is doing and teaching things that only someone sent by God could. But who is he, really? Instead of discussing his identity, Jesus changes the subject: "Truly I tell you, unless someone is born again, he cannot see the kingdom of God," he says (John 3:3).

Nicodemus is confused. After all, how can a person who is already born be born *again*? What does that even mean? And for that matter, why do we need to be?

Here's the big idea of what Jesus was getting at: to be born again is to be given new life by the Holy Spirit, who, like Jesus, is also God but is not Jesus. It's complicated, but Christians believe that there is one God who created everything and that this one God exists simultaneously as three distinct persons—God the Father, God the Son (Jesus), and God the Holy Spirit. The Father, Son, and Spirit are all fully and equally God, with none lesser or greater than the others, but are not one another. Throughout the New Testament, you see these three interact with one another in different ways, such as in Jesus's baptism (Matthew 3:13–17). If you're still confused, don't worry—you're in good company.

According to the story of the Bible, humanity has a problem called sin, which is the wrong things we do and the right things we don't do. This problem affects everything about us—what we desire, what we believe, who we think we are. *Everything.* It also puts us at odds with God because what we want, believe,

3

and think as people affected and shaped by sin is opposed to the One who made everything. The Bible calls people left to our own devices dead in our sins (Ephesians 2:1), dying physically day by day, and existing in a perpetual state of spiritual death with no desire to love, honor, or worship God at all.

But when we believe in Jesus, everything changes. Belief, in this sense, is an act that goes beyond merely acknowledging Jesus's existence (something even demons do, according to James 2:19) to trusting that what Jesus did in dying and rising again really happened and that he did it for us. Believing in Jesus is an act of faith. Through that faith—itself a gift from God (Ephesians 2:8)—we are born again, made alive with Christ (Ephesians 2:5). The old you is gone. No more. Done.

This is why you are a new you that is still you, but not. A new you brought about by a new birth that gives you new desires, a new purpose, a new identity, and a new future:

- **New desires:** you actually want the things God wants (Psalm 37:4; Philippians 2:13).

- **New purpose:** your whole life is meant to be about honoring, enjoying, and serving him (Psalm 73:24–26; John 17:22, 24; 1 Corinthians 10:31; Romans 11:36).

- **New identity:** you are a beloved child adopted into the family of God, and your Father is God himself, and your older brother is Jesus Christ (Ephesians 1:5).

- **New future:** you are destined to live forever with God in a renewed and restored world (Revelation 21:1–22:5).

Y'know, little things like that.

STARTING FROM SCRATCH

What we experience before the age of five has a major influence on what happens through the rest of our lives.[2] This time in our lives *really* mattered. In fact, it's no stretch to say we are who we are in many ways because of what we experienced during those years. The same is true in our faith. Just as the early years of a child's development are the most crucial, so too are our early years as Christians. In a very real way, when you become a Christian, especially when you're coming to faith as an adult, you're starting life over from scratch. You're a grown-up in body, but a child in your faith, which means these early weeks, months, and years *are* a crucial time in your faith.

This is not meant to be insulting. Everyone who believes in Jesus starts out that way, no matter how old they are when they first believe. You are a new person, and because of that you are, at least when it comes to your faith, kind of like a child: a sponge, open to learning all you can, free to ask any question you want (something, I suspect, more established Christians might even be a bit jealous of). What you learn now will shape a great deal of your experience as a follower of Jesus going forward. This is no exaggeration. I went through it, too.

THE MESS JESUS MADE
WHEN HE SAVED ME

I didn't grow up in a Christian home. We were, more or less, your typical Canadian secular, single-parent family. There was no expectation of going to church. We didn't read the Bible. We

---

2. These are the years where we learn about our identity, develop our sense of dignity and value, hopefully stop picking our noses in public, learn social skills, and so much more. See "Your Child's Development," ChildCare.gov, https://childcare.gov/consumer-education/your-childs-development.

didn't pray. We didn't do much of anything that touched on the spiritual side of reality. And I didn't really have a problem with that because God wasn't on my radar.

As a teen, I started dipping my toe into Eastern philosophy and mysticism. This wasn't because I was looking for any sort of fulfillment. I just wanted to impress girls with how deep I was. (It didn't work.) Later, in college, I met a girl named Emily. She was smart, pretty (and I mean *really* pretty), and was into this religion called Bahá'í, which teaches that the figures of all the world's major religions were part of a long chain of revelation from God, with their messages being authoritative for their specific time and place. Their founder, naturally, said he was the one to bring the revelation from God that would usher in an era of peace and prosperity for humanity, which his successor would lead. I went to a few of their events with Emily because, well, she was *really* pretty. For whatever reason, she liked me. After a while, she decided she'd rather spend her time with a borderline-nihilist agnostic than continue down the road of obligatory prayers, regular fasting, and ritual handwashing, because eventually she wasn't a Bahá'í anymore.

Then, in 2004, God decided it was time for me to get to know him. I was home from work sick one day and decided to open an online messaging program (this was in the days before social media and widespread texting). My friend Adam asked whether I wanted to go to this thing at his church called Alpha, where you share a high-carb meal, watch a video, and discuss matters of faith. To his surprise, and mine, I said yes, registered, and forgot what it was about. When Emily came home from work, I mentioned I'd signed us up to go to some dinner discussion group thing at Adam's church. Her response was, "Cool, free food."

Then we arrived and were surprised to find that it was a ten-week course.[3]

We went dutifully every week. We ate the high-carb food. We watched the videos (or rather, Emily did; I fell asleep as soon as the lights went down, but my ignorance didn't prevent me from engaging in the discussion afterward). Some people became Christians. One couple even got married during Alpha, with everyone's invitation to the ceremony issued moments before it began. And as we watched the happy couple say their "I do's," the high-carb meal for the night transformed into an equally high-carb—but cost-effective—wedding reception.

At the end of the course, we said, "That's nice. We're glad we know what our friend believes." And we went on our merry way.

But God wasn't done with either of us just yet.

Despite the failure of Alpha to win me to Jesus, Adam kept talking to us about faith. Then on one Saturday afternoon in March 2005, I decided, "If I'm going to keep making fun of Christianity, I should make sure I do it knowledgeably." So, I went to the Christian bookstore two blocks from the house Emily and I had recently purchased, bought a Bible, and (despite having been told to start with John's Gospel) started reading Mark and Luke. I was blown away by what I was reading—the Jesus I saw there wasn't the Buddy Christ of Kevin Smith's *Dogma*, the blasphemous Jesus of *Family Guy*, the slot-machine Jesus of the prosperity-preaching fools on TV, or even the mythical/mystical but misguided good teacher Jesus of agnostics, atheists,

---

3. The Alpha program, developed in the United Kingdom, explores the fundamental beliefs of the Christian faith. It has since spawned many similar programs to engage non-Christians in meaningful discussion about the basics of Christian belief in a safe, no-pressure environment.

and secular humanists. This was a man I *had* to take seriously. I couldn't *not*.

At the same time as I began to wrestle with the question of who Jesus was, we were brought face-to-face with the reality that we live in a supernatural world. After around 10 p.m., there were rooms Emily and I avoided, such as our bathroom. It always seemed like something, someone, was present. Emily described me as fighting in my sleep (something I had never done before). I'd wake up with scratches I couldn't have made. Emily kept getting phone calls where there was nothing coming through the line. This went on for weeks. It finally came to a head in the middle of the night in early June 2005, when something picked me up out of bed.

Emily saw what was happening and screamed. That's when I dropped like a rock.

I was scared. I didn't know what to do. So I tried something I had done only one other time in my adult life: I prayed. "Ummm, God? If you're even real, and if this is real, can you let me know?"

It got worse.

I was pinned to the bed, with what felt like a two-hundred-pound man sitting on my chest. I tried to move but couldn't. I tried to speak but had no words. I didn't know what was happening exactly. I only wanted it to stop. But there wasn't anything I could do—not on my own, anyway.

Out of nowhere, I remembered some of what I had read about Jesus. He had power over these things. He could make this stop. I only had to ask. But I knew that I had to not only ask him to save me from what I was experiencing but ask him to save *me*—to forgive me for all of the sins I had committed. To forgive me for not believing he was even real.

And he did.

Right there, in the same bed I'd fallen into moments before, right next to Emily, who'd experienced her own dramatic conversion literally seconds before me.[4] After a few moments of dumbfounded silence, we looked at one another and said, "Now what?"

HOW DO YOU MAKE SENSE OF THE MESS?

Up to that point, we had been a typical non-Christian couple: we'd been living together for about four years, had been engaged for two and a half, owned a home and car. Now, everything we'd been taught and assumed had to be examined, sometimes for the very first time.

But God was kind to us. We joined a church right away, one that God used during that time to bring a number of couples in similar situations to ours to himself, including my friend Adam. We met very kind people. The pastor took a particular interest in me—partly because I questioned him about a controversial issue the first time we attended a service. Despite kind of flying by the seat of his pants (because we all were), he did his best to help us navigate the mess of our lives. And make no mistake: Emily and I were *giant* messes.

Chances are, you're feeling that way (about yourself). You've lived your whole life to this point doing more or less what you pleased. Now, you're trying to figure out what it means to be a Christian when you've never been one before and may never have seen an example of one. While you're hopefully involved in a local church and you've started to develop some relationships, it's also likely that many of the people you are getting to know, people who want to encourage and help you along your journey, won't really know the best way to do that.

---

4. You can read her story: Emily Armstrong, "From the Bahá'í Faith to Porn to Alpha to Jesus," *Christianity Today* (October 2015), https://www.christianitytoday.com/ct/2015/october/from-bahai-faith-to-porn-to-alpha-to-jesus.html.

Many more established Christians and churches struggle to know how to best support you because your experiences and environments are foreign to them. Many grew up with believing parents who deeply loved Jesus and encouraged worshiping him. To many, especially those from areas where elements of Christianity haunt the culture (such as the US South), Christianity seems normal (kind of like it does to my own kids, which is still weird to me). The habits, the symbols, and the language of Christianity are generally understood without much, if any, explanation.

But for those of us who grew up without any real connection with—or, in some cases, awareness of—Christianity, there is nothing normal about it. We don't see a cross and think "Jesus." We see a cross and see the letter *t*.

And we're not alone. Our numbers are only increasing in places such as the United States, Canada, and England, as those countries become increasingly ignorant of Christianity.[5] As our numbers increase, it's going to become even more difficult for many Christians and churches to know what to do with us—both before and after coming to faith in Jesus.

That's where this book comes in.

NAVIGATING THE "NOW WHAT" OF YOUR FAITH

One of my wife's oldest friends never emails. She doesn't call, and she doesn't text either. She always sends letters. I asked my wife once what it was about—this low-tech, slow, and kind of expensive way of communicating that brings her and her friend

---

5. Kristy Etheridge, "The Vanishing Bible Belt: The Secrets Southern Churches Must Learn to Stay Healthy," Lifeway Research, February 3, 2021, https://research.lifeway.com/2021/02/03/the-vanishing-bible-belt-the-secrets-southern-churches-must-learn-to-stay-healthy.

so much joy. She told me it's just more personal. That's how I want you to think about this book—as a letter from me to you. I want to help guide you out of the mess of being an adult new believer, navigating you around some of the land mines that you might otherwise step on (and a few I did) toward a healthy faith in Jesus.

In this book, you'll learn about important habits you need to develop and know why they matter, such as reading the Bible and praying. You'll learn how to recognize a healthy church. I'll try to address some big questions about practical living, such as navigating romantic relationships (especially if the one you're in predates your faith) and figuring out how to disagree on big and small issues in a way that reflects your faith in Jesus. I'll also give some guidance on things that might seem silly—like how to read good books and listen to good music—but that actually make a huge difference in your life once you know how they relate to your faith. You'll even learn about a few important truths of the Christian faith along the way.

These things will shape the next five, ten, and maybe fifty years of your life. The answers you get from me will not be perfect. I'm still on the path myself, even if it's a few steps ahead. But I hope that what I've learned in those few steps will be a help to you as you take your next one.

ABSOLUTE BEGINNERS

//

INTRODUCING THE OBVIOUS PARTS OF THE CHRISTIAN LIFE (THAT AREN'T ALL THAT OBVIOUS)

Christianity is weird. We believe that there is a God we can't see— one who exists outside space and time and made everything in the universe. We believe this same God sent his Son, Jesus (who is also God), into the world to live and die and live again for us. We believe that when we believe Jesus did this, our sins are forgiven forever, and that someday this very same Jesus is coming back to fix the mess of this world.

Many Christians—especially those who grew up in Christian homes—forget how weird all this is. They also forget how equally weird much of what they know about being a Christian is, especially for those of us without any church background:

We read a book written thousands of years ago to learn about God.

We close our eyes and talk out loud and make requests of God.

We get together and sing songs to and about God.[1]

We go around telling other people about this God so they
can come and do all these weird things with us, too.

Christians forget about the weirdness of this because many
fall prey to the curse of knowledge The idea behind this is that
people who are very familiar with any type of information—
whether it is cooking an egg, changing a car's oil, or designing a
rocket—can wrongly assume that their knowledge is common.
Except it isn't.[2] They don't do it out of any malice, of course. It's
just that they assume everyone knows the basics.

So in this and the following chapters, I don't want to make
any assumptions about what you have been taught about the
basic practices that many Christians see as givens. These practices are habits that help you grow in your faith, and they are
ones you want to develop early and keep a priority in your life,
no matter what.[3] They require a certain kind of grit at different
periods of your life (believe me) and sometimes don't seem like
they make all that much of a difference in the moment. But over
weeks, months, and years, they are life changing. Here are the
primary habits you need to commit to, with God's help:

1. Regularly reading the Bible.

2. Praying.

---

1. Although some of those songs also sound like they could be about one of your parents,
   or possibly a boyfriend or girlfriend. That may be the weirdest part of all.
2. This concept is described in detail in Chip Heath and Dan Heath's book *Made to
   Stick: Why Some Ideas Survive and Others Die* (New York: Random House, 2007).
3. Sometimes these are called spiritual disciplines, which can sound rigid and restrictive.
   But spiritual disciplines are simply habits or practices designed to help us develop
   and grow in our faith.

3. Having a community of other Christians where you know them deeply and they know you deeply.

More established Christians might read this list and say, "Well, I should hope so." That's fine. After all, I wasn't exaggerating when I said these would be considered obvious by many. But here's the thing: even though they *are* obvious, very few professing Christians do them on a consistent basis. Only a few American Christians read their Bibles on a daily basis; most read it, at best, once a week, which probably means that they're reading whatever text is being taught in their church on Sunday.[4] People pray, but few know *how* to pray or whether it matters at all. Where at least weekly was the norm a generation ago, today if you go to church once a month you're considered a regular attender.[5]

So why these habits? Why are these disciplines the ones I'm calling out? While there are others, these are the pillars—the legs of the stool that is the Christian life. If you lose one, the stool is unsound, and if you try to sit on it, you'll come crashing down. That's why I want to make sure you're grounded in them. I want you to have a strong foundation that will help you stand up to the trials, difficulties, and dumpster fires that will come your way in the years to come (because they will). In this chapter, we'll talk about the first leg of the stool—reading the Bible regularly.

4. According to Barna Research, 14 percent of American Christians read the Bible every day in 2019. See "Signs of Decline and Hope among Key Metrics of Faith," Barna Group, March 4, 2020, https://www.barna.com/research/changing-state-of-the-church/. Lifeway Research reported slightly less discouraging findings, but theirs are still concerning. See Aaron Earls, "Few Protestant Churchgoers Read the Bible Daily," Lifeway Research, July 2, 2019, https://research.lifeway.com/2019/07/02/few-protestant-churchgoers-read-the-bible-daily.
5. "Signs of Decline and Hope"; "Few Protestant Churchgoers Read the Bible Daily."

READING THE BIBLE: DELIGHT
OR DRUDGERY (OR BOTH?)

I am a reader. I regularly read an average of two books every week. I have thousands of books in my house and thousands more available in various apps and tools. But out of all of them, the one that is the most important to me is the Bible. My favorite Bible is a beat-up, marked-up copy I purchased a couple of years after coming to faith. Some pages are hard to read because of all my notes and highlights. Chunks of pleather are falling off the cover. It looks like it may have been run over by a car at one point. It's the Bible I have absolutely destroyed with use. I loved it to death, the way that my children did with their special blankets when they were toddlers. It's a Bible that reminds me how I want to see reading the Bible: as a delight!

Part of whether you consider reading the Bible a delight is connected to how much you *enjoy* reading. Regardless of how *much* you read, if reading is a pleasure for you, delight is probably a word that will resonate with you. But if you've avoided picking up a book since the last one you were assigned in school, reading is probably the furthest thing from a delight you could imagine. Drudgery might be a better way to describe it. And whether you love or hate reading, it can be both. There are times when you delight in it, and there are others when it's a challenge to even pick the Bible up, let alone read a single line. While there are many reasons for this, one might be that there is a conflict between what we see in the Bible and how we are often taught to read it.

WHAT THE BIBLE IS

Before we can talk about the best way to read the Bible, then, I want to make sure you understand what the Bible is.

The Bible is—and is not—a single book. The single book we call the Bible today is a collection of books and letters, the earliest of which were written about thirty-five hundred years ago or so.[6] These books and letters are written in different styles and genres, each with a distinct intent by their authors. Some books, such as Joshua, Judges, 1–2 Samuel, 1–2 Kings, 1–2 Chronicles, Esther, Ezra, and Nehemiah, are intended to be read as historical narratives. Others, such as the Psalms, are a collection of hymns, songs, and prayers written, spoken, and sung to God. In many ways, Psalms is the most human book of the Bible, expressing the full array of thoughts and emotions people expressed to God in the midst of times of both blessing and trial. Others still are prophetic books, which sometimes include narrative strands and poetic language, but with the purpose of revealing a specific message from God and often glimpses into the (then) future. There's more I could say about different genres within the Bible's collected writing (and I didn't even touch the books with strange images of swords and lampstands and many-horned beasts), but let's keep going. Even though the Bible is a collection of different writings, it is also one book that communicates a single message. (We'll get to that message in a bit.)

The Bible is consistent and trustworthy. The Bible was written over thousands of years by dozens of individuals. Normally, you would expect a book like that to be disjointed and confusing. But instead, it is remarkably consistent. One way Christian teachers commonly put it is that it is free from error,

6. The first five books of the Bible—Genesis, Exodus, Leviticus, Numbers, and Deuteronomy—are traditionally believed to have been written by Moses, who lived somewhere between the 1500s and 1300s BC. You may wonder, though, how Moses could have written the last chapters of Deuteronomy when he dies in them. These are believed to have been written by his assistant, Joshua, who was kind of a big deal in Numbers, Deuteronomy, and Joshua.

internal conflict, or contradiction.[7] They call this the *inerrancy* of Scripture. The primary reason for this consistency comes from what Christians believe about how the Bible was written. We believe that the human authors who wrote the Bible did so with the help of God himself, which is what we mean when we say that the Bible is *inspired*.

That help came, typically, in one of two ways. Sometimes God directly gave them the words to write (saying, "Write this down," as in Exodus 17:14; Deuteronomy 31:19; Ezekiel 24:2; and Habakkuk 2:2). More frequently, the Holy Spirit worked through human beings to communicate what both the human author and God intended (2 Peter 1:21), using author's personality, perspective, and grammatical peculiarities.

All this said, the inerrancy and inspiration of the Bible do not apply to Bible translations, such as the one you own. They apply only to the original writings, those first written by their authors, thousands of years ago. What we have available to us today are translations based on copies of the originals. But even then, we don't have to wonder whether what you and I read is inaccurate or untrustworthy (even if you find yourself questioning a translation decision or two as time goes on). Even though translators make mistakes sometimes, they work hard to communicate the message of the text as faithfully and clearly

---

7. There are some passages people will point to suggesting that there are contradictions within the Bible, but if we study them closely and charitably, we find the contradictions are apparent rather than real. For example, James 2:14–26 and Romans 4:1–5:5 point to the same verse in the Old Testament (Genesis 15:6, "Abram believed the Lord, and *God* credited it to him as righteousness") to make seemingly opposite points. But Romans 4–5 is part of a larger exploration of the gospel itself and how we are not made right with God through anything we do but only his grace. James 2 doesn't deny this but is addressing a different issue entirely, that our faith is demonstrated in what we do. Another way to say it is that we are not saved by works, but our works reveal that we are saved.

as possible. The copies of the original writings that we have, in part and in whole, encompass thousands of copies made by hand over thousands of years. You might think this would lead to a lot of mistakes, but when we compare the copies we have to one another, there is a remarkable degree of consistency. The disagreements that do appear are overwhelmingly typos, such as transposed letters (think "their" and "thier"). There are a few passages where there are substantial disagreements between copies, but they don't fundamentally alter the message of the Bible.

How is this even possible? Ultimately, the most accurate explanation is one that, prior to your becoming a Christian, would have been the least intellectually satisfying to you: God *preserved* it through the generations, preventing the words of the Bible from becoming corrupted to such a degree that we can, with good confidence, trust that the message our Bibles contain today is the same message the original authors intended.

The Bible is meant to be understood. God wasn't trying to be obscure when he inspired the Bible. This means that we can use the basic rules we intuitively use when reading anything else, whether a novel, blog post, biography, or history book. Figurative language (similes, metaphors, analogies, and so forth) should be read that way unless there's a compelling reason not to. When read the way we would read any other book, we generally find that the message of the Bible is clear and can easily be understood. The term used for this is the clarity, or *perspicuity*, of Scripture, which means that the Bible was written in such a way that its core message can be understood by the average person. But regardless of this, know that you can understand the Bible. Where something is unclear, there are plenty of resources to help bring the clarity you need, starting with the introductions to each book found in most Bibles.

So that's what the Bible *is* from a mechanics standpoint—what it is on a technical level and how it was written. But there are a few things the Bible is *not* that you need to understand so you can read it as it was intended.

First, the Bible is not an instruction manual. People who love acronyms sometimes refer to the Bible as "Basic Instructions Before Living Eternally." The idea behind this is that the Bible is intended to instruct us on how we are to live in the world now while we wait for Jesus to return. We read the Bible to know how we are supposed to live in the world. And while the Bible does have very clear commands within its pages, it isn't an instruction manual. It is much, *much* more than that. (Remember that single message? Yeah, that—we'll get there.)

Second, the Bible is not a collection of ancient morality tales. The Bible has some pretty amazing characters in it. We see examples of great faith, of courage, and of overcoming adversity. But if we read the Bible just looking at the people in it as examples, we wind up reading it as though it were on the same level as Aesop's Fables—something from which we can draw moral wisdom. The people in the Bible were real, and so they had flaws. If we read the Bible as a collection of morality tales, we can lose the realness of the people about whom we read. The Bible isn't meant for that; it's meant for something much more. (Keep waiting.)

Third, the Bible is not a repository of inspirational sayings. You've probably noticed that many Christians tend to talk about or share Bible verses in isolation. It's not at all uncommon to see verses such as Jeremiah 29:11 ("For I know the plans I have for you ... plans for your well-being, not for disaster, to give you a future and a hope"); John 3:16 ("For God loved the world in this way: he gave his one and only Son so that everyone who believes in him will not perish but have eternal life"); or Philippians 4:13

("I am able to do all things through him who strengthens me") on wall art, coffee cups, social media profiles, and bumper stickers. There's a good reason for this: these verses have inspired believers for generations! There's just one problem: when we read them in isolation, apart from the rest of Scripture, including their immediate context, we treat them as simple inspirational sayings, truisms, and well-meaning platitudes from which we gain a little spiritual pick-me-up rather than life-changing truth. And while there's nothing wrong with a pick-me-up now and then, if this is the only way we interact with the Bible, we're more likely to misunderstand its message.

WHAT THE BIBLE IS ABOUT

So, if the Bible isn't a rule book, and if it's not a collection of morality tales, and it isn't a big book of inspirational sayings, then what is it, really? That was one of the questions that plagued me as a new believer. Reading the Bible, I was equal parts amazed and confused by it. I could understand what I was reading, but I didn't really have a good sense of how to put it all together. (I was also a bit dumb and decided to tackle several not-so-easy-to-understand books, such as Revelation, right out of the chute.) And although my pastors at the time were wonderful people who aimed to be faithful in what they taught, how they taught didn't help much with this. They primarily taught principles from the Bible, with a typical sermon including several verse references beneath each point, much like what you've already seen periodically in this chapter. It's not an invalid way of teaching, but it is a style that can treat the Bible the ways I just described—as a rule book, as morality tales, and as inspirational sayings. The natural result is that I would walk away every week wondering what I was supposed to do after reading the Bible. It essentially made the Bible about *me* instead of what it's truly about.

I know I've been teasing this for a while, so, finally, it's time to tell you what the Bible is all about, from beginning to end:

The Bible is about God.

Okay, that's a bit vague. It's about God, but it's not about God in general. It's about God's plan to rescue and restore—or, to redeem—his creation through the death, burial, and resurrection of Jesus. From Genesis to Revelation, that's what the Bible is all about. It's about the good news (the meaning of the word gospel) that God has a plan to redeem creation through Jesus. What helped me see that was a moment in the Gospel of John.

In John 5, Jesus confronts a group of Jewish teachers called the Pharisees, some of the most influential religious leaders of his day. These were the guys who were super serious about obeying the Scriptures, particularly the law, which governed the moral, civil, and ceremonial aspects of Jewish culture (which is to say, everything). Their motto, essentially, was, "Follow the law, no matter what." They had a good reason for taking this approach: they knew the history of their people. God had made them a great nation, a people meant to be a shining light to draw people to God. But the problem was that they, like the rest of us, were sinners. In other words, they didn't consistently obey God, and truth be told, they didn't want to. After centuries of a repeating cycle of rebellion, rejection, and restoration, the people were sent into captivity in a land called Babylon for seventy years. When they returned to their homeland, they vowed to never rebel against God again.

So they became incredibly diligent about studying their Bible, which we call the Old Testament. But in their diligence, they missed something important—or rather, *someone* important. Someone God promised to send into the world to save his people, a promised king called the Messiah or Christ. But when they met that someone, they viewed him as a problem. He didn't follow the law the way they expected him (and everyone else) to. He violated the law, according to their understanding of it, by doing things such as healing the sick—and even having the audacity to do it on the Sabbath, the Jewish people's holy day of rest.

That someone, if you hadn't guessed, was Jesus.

So in John 5, the Pharisees confront Jesus about what he is doing. But Jesus is having none of it. After telling them that he is only doing what his Father—God—is doing (John 5:17), and then rebuking them for failing to understand what they are seeing and what Jesus is doing (19–38), he completely shatters their understanding of the Bible with one statement: "You pore over the Scriptures because you think you have eternal life in them, and yet they testify about me" (John 5:39).

The first time I read that sentence, I missed what Jesus was saying. But then I read it again. And then I read Luke 24:27, where Jesus explains how the Old Testament points to him.[8] So I started to read passages from the Old Testament that were quoted in the New—the ones the authors themselves used in reference to Jesus—such as Isaiah 61:1–2 (Luke 4:18–19); Psalm 22 (Matthew 27:35, 39, 46; Mark 15:24, 34; Luke 23:34–35; John 19:23–24; Hebrews 2:11–12); and Numbers 21:4–19 (John 3:14–15).[9] As I read, I got it. Jesus wasn't using hyperbole when he said that the Scriptures testify about him. They actually do—he is the connecting thread that runs throughout every book of the Bible. The Bible is the story of God's plan to send Jesus to rescue his

8. The phrase "beginning with Moses and all the Prophets" used by Luke is a way of saying the entire Old Testament. Jesus likely would have shown this both through explicit passages and historical patterns.
9. This article offers a great starting point on where we can see Jesus in the Old Testament: Karen Engle, "Where's Jesus in the Old Testament? Start with These 12 Verses," Word by Word, November 19, 2019, https://blog.logos.com/wheres-jesus-in-the-old-testament-start-with-these-12-verses/. A great book that addresses this topic more deeply is Edmund Clowney, *The Unfolding Mystery* (Phillipsburg, NJ: P&R, 2013).

people from sin. When I got that, it changed everything about how I read the Bible, even as a new believer.

The Old Testament as the foundation. I started to recognize that the Old Testament is the foundation for the gospel. It's where, even as God exists in and before the beginning (Genesis 1:1), Jesus exists in the beginning with God—the Word through whom and for whom everything is created (John 1:1). It's where the first promise of redemption and restoration is given after the first sin (Genesis 3:15). It's where the promise of blessing to all nations through the offspring of one man—an elderly man named Abraham—is given (Genesis 12:1–3). Where faith is tested (Genesis 22:1–19). Where belief is declared righteousness (Genesis 15:6). Where God rescues a people from captivity who cannot save themselves and makes them his people (Exodus 1–20). Where kingdoms rise and fall, the wise become fools, and kings become captives (1–2 Samuel; 1–2 Kings). Where, even after failure upon failure from generation to generation, God says, "I will come" (Malachi 4:6).

Seeing the Old Testament in this way even makes us love a book like Leviticus, helping us see the depth of Jesus's love for us in that he fulfilled every command in that book, giving us a deeper appreciation of his words, "It is finished" (John 19:30).

The New Testament as good news. This change didn't just affect how I read the Old Testament; it changed how I looked at the New. When we read the Bible like an instruction manual, we can turn the New Testament into a new law. We do it with everything, including the Beatitudes, with their declaration of who belongs in the kingdom of God (Matthew 5:3–10). We can try to make them a list of behaviors, asking ourselves, "Am I poor in spirit enough today? Did I make enough peace?" We take what the Holy Spirit does within us, which is to grow in us "love, joy, peace, patience, kindness, goodness, faithfulness, gentleness, and self-control" (Galatians 5:22–23), and try to make it a goal

ABSOLUTE BEGINNERS

to white-knuckle our way forward. We take the descriptions of the early church in Acts 2 and 3 and assume that the believers selling all their possessions and sharing all they had is a specific instruction, rather than a description of the beauty of the gospel at work in the lives of God's people. But the New Testament isn't a new law. It is good news. It is where we see how Christ completed the law for us and how by faith, his righteousness, his completion of the law, he becomes ours. God gives us grace, and we live in response to it.

The good news that changes our lives today. One of the things that I love most about this understanding of the Bible—that it is the story of God's plan to rescue and redeem the world—is that we know how it ends. It ends with a promise: "I am coming soon" (Revelation 22:20). This is such good news. Jesus is coming back, and when he does, sin will be no more, and death will die, and God's people will rejoice. Jesus will wipe every tear from every eye of every one of us. Jesus cares deeply for every single one of his people, and he will comfort each of us when he makes all things new. In other words, we know there's no question over whether Jesus will be victorious. We know that there's no doubt that he will return, even if we don't know when that is. But he gives us confidence that he will be coming soon. And we have the opportunity to share this hope with others while we wait for soon to become now.

That's what helps us to live faithfully in the moment. One of the running themes of life in this world—no matter where or when we live—is fear and uncertainty. Concerns about health, employment (or lack thereof), personal relationships, wars and rumors of wars, conspiracy theories, and political division weigh heavily on us. Media of all forms thrives on being the bearers of bad news, always ready to add a cloud to your silver lining. Because fear and uncertainty are the air in which we live and breathe, it's tempting to lose hope, and become resigned to living in fear. But this isn't what God has intended for us. He has shown us how the story ends—and it is good news! That good news changes everything.

HOW TO READ YOUR BIBLE

We've talked about what the Bible is, what it isn't, and what it is all about. That might seem like a lot to go through when we're supposed to be talking about reading the Bible regularly. But if you don't know this, you'll have a problem. You might dutifully read the Bible on a somewhat regular basis. You might be inspired periodically. You might be encouraged. You might find yourself thinking you can do all things through a verse taken out of context. But you'll be missing the thing that makes the Bible so radically life changing—that makes it a delight. That being said, I do want to make sure you have a helpful framework for how to read Scripture.

Use a translation that works for you. There are so many translations available, and they use different translation philosophies:

Some lean toward a word-for-word method, attempting to minimize interpretation within translation for the sake of accuracy. The ESV (English Standard Version), the NASB (New American Standard Bible), and the KJV (King James Version) are all commonly used translations that generally take this approach. Of these, the ESV is my typical go-to, particularly for study purposes, although it can be a little opaque at times.

Others take a more thought-for-thought approach, prioritizing the clarity of meaning versus strict adherence to the words used in the original languages. Bibles taking this approach include the CSB (Christian Standard Bible), NET (New English Translation), NIV (New International Version), and the NLT (New Living Translation). These are extremely helpful for gaining clarity around core ideas, but this approach can some-times lean too heavily toward paraphrase rather than proper translation. Within this translation approach, the CSB and NET are among the best, and these are my preferred translations for personal reading and teaching.

But whatever approach you prefer, pick a Bible you're going to want to read on a regular basis. If you don't, you won't.

Read a little every day. There are some great and helpful plans out there to help you set and attain a reasonable goal for reading the Bible. One of the most popular today is one devel-oped by a nineteenth-century Scottish pastor named Robert Murray M'Cheyne, which takes the approach of reading through the entirety of the Old Testament once and the New Testament and Psalms twice. It's a good program, but I don't know that I would use that to start, if only because it's a demanding one. (But if you're up for the challenge, do it!) Other solid plans include chronological ones that take you through the Bible roughly in order of when events happened. There are other plans built around major themes as well. But the big idea is this: whatever approach you take, it needs to be attainable and play to your strengths (which include your reading comfort and comprehension). If you've got time for reading five to ten minutes a day, you're set. Eventually you'll get to the end. (And then you can start again.)

Take notes. Write what stands out to you. Underline and circle important words. Look for connections to other passages as you read. This helps you get a better sense of how the Bible all fits together. Don't be afraid to mark up your Bible—interacting with it physically will help you remember what you read and help you to come back to passages that are meaningful to you.

Pray as you read. By this, I mean don't just pray before or after you read (which is wise to do), but when you're reading, stop whenever you need clarity and ask God for understanding. When you feel like reading is a chore, pray and ask God to help you to enjoy it. When you find something that amazes you, pray and thank God for that wonderful gift!

Expect that you'll hear from God as you read. Because of our beliefs about God inspiring the Bible, Christians come to it with an expectation that we will hear from God. We believe this is the primary way that God speaks to us—it's how he reveals his nature and character, his plans for the world, and the hope we have in Jesus. It doesn't tell us everything about how the world works, but it tells us everything we need to live as faithful followers of Jesus today.

KEEPING THE BIBLE YOUR PRIORITY

I feel like a bit of a hypocrite writing this chapter. I constantly struggle to maintain a healthy practice of reading the Bible. I've had times when I've let reading books *about* the Bible or about issues related to the Christian faith take the place of reading the Bible itself. But here's the truth: there is no substitute for reading the Bible. You really do yourself a disservice—and even put yourself in spiritual harm—if the Bible is not your priority. And I know, because I've seen what happens when you don't.

I became a Christian at a time when most of the popular Christian authors and teachers were focused on asking lots of questions but seemed to give few answers. My friends and I would read books that were filled with deep theological problems that we couldn't yet recognize. We were enamored by the idea of people rebelling, even though they were rebelling against something we knew nothing about (since none of us grew up in the American evangelical subculture). We talked about questions and doubts and mystery. We listened to lectures on reclaiming the way of Jesus by focusing less on personal holiness and more on social issues like alleviating poverty, reducing our carbon footprints, and education reform.[10]

But as we did that, you know what we weren't doing? We weren't building a solid foundation based on reading our Bibles, at least not to the degree that we ought to have. And when we did have Bible studies, we weren't trying to understand what Paul meant when he wrote Romans or 1 Corinthians. We weren't really digging into the Sermon on the Mount or considering carefully what it meant to abide in Jesus like branches on a vine as he told us to in John 15. Instead, we took a very me-focused approach, asking one another what the Bible meant to us personally without thinking about what its authors intended or what it meant to its original audience. We were like hyperactive kids after an intense game of ring-around-the-rosie: we worked ourselves up into a tizzy and then all fell down.

Some of us never got up again.

What I understand now, and wish I'd understood then, is that even though there's a place for discussing serious questions, and books can be a great blessing (even the bad ones, if you know what to look for), the most important thing we can do as new believers is ground ourselves in the Bible. We need to prioritize reading it regularly because it tells us of our great God and Savior, Jesus Christ; it contains the good news of his death and resurrection and the promise of his return; and it informs us of the world's greatest need and its only hope.

10. This is a false dichotomy. Christians don't—and shouldn't—have to choose between pursuing personal holiness and addressing the real needs of the world. This is something I wrote about at length in *Awaiting a Savior: The Gospel, The New Creation, and the End of Poverty* (Minneapolis: Cruciform Press, 2011).

The Bible is the foundation of our life as Christians. Get a grip on it now. Don't let anything else take away from its priority in your life. Do this, and it will go well for you.

ABSOLUTE BEGINNERS

29

HAVE A TALK WITH GOD

//

HOW TO PRAY WITHOUT IT FEELING WEIRD

"Um, okay, God? I'm not sure you're even real. But if you are ..."

Those were the first words I remember ever praying. It was in my backyard at around 1 a.m., still at least a couple of weeks before Jesus saved me.

We had gotten home late after spending the night hanging out with a Christian couple we met through our friend Adam. Through the night, we had great conversations about everything you can imagine: life, family history, work, even Jesus. They were curious about what we'd read in our Bibles. Emily talked a lot about the different experiences she had as a Baha'i as well as some of the different spiritual practices and beliefs she was exposed to growing up. Most of it was the New Age–y stuff that permeated the Oprah Winfrey show and books by guys like Gary Zukav and Deepak Chopra. But she also saw a family member or two use tarot cards and different apparently harmless novelty items sold to engage with the supernatural world. In her post-Baha'i existence, she got a set of her own cards. She used them once in a while, but usually, they collected dust on a shelf.

As we drove home, we reflected on the conversations we had, and out of the blue, Emily said, "We need to get rid of the tarot cards."

"Cool," I said. "Do you want to throw them out?"

"No. I think I need to burn them."

So that's what we were doing in my backyard. We grabbed a pan from the kitchen, lined it with foil, put the cards and their box inside, threw in some newspaper to help get a fire started, and lit a match. Except the dang things didn't burn.

That's when I started to pray my feeble, uncertain first prayer. I have no idea what prompted me to do it. No one told me to. It just seemed like the right thing to do, even though I still wasn't sure whether God was really even real.

Barely a breath after I finished saying, "Do you think you could maybe make these things burn?"—fwoosh! Up in flames they went.

Despite my uncertainty, God was kind to answer. That's how he is.

God is relational. That means he didn't make us and then leave us to our own devices. He is involved in our world and with us. He makes his existence known through what he has made; his nature and power—his "invisible attributes," as Romans 1:20 puts it—are visible in everything he has made. He speaks to us through the Bible. He even came into the world to live among human beings, taking on humanity when Jesus was born (Philippians 2:5–7)! And he hears us. He listens to us. How?

Primarily, through *prayer*.

WHAT IS PRAYER?

Prayer is the second of three essential habits of the Christian life that ground us in our faith. The shortest way to define it is that *prayer is talking to God and developing a personal connection with him.* That's it. No qualifications or caveats needed. Prayer is talking to God. The amazing thing is that you can talk to him about anything: specific needs that you or others have, what you're feeling. You can also just talk to him, much like a child does with a parent. And remember, if you are a Christian, God is your Father, so this isn't an analogy stretched too thin. (Also, how mind blowing is that?) However, this analogy is also one that is difficult for many people to fully understand, especially those of us who come from families with unhealthy dynamics or abusive households. It is tempting to project our understanding and experience of father on God instead of allowing the truth of Scripture to correct our understanding. This can take a long time, and in many cases, a great deal of counseling, so if you chafe at the analogy, please know that you are not alone.

While prayer is, first and foremost, talking to God, it is also *one of God's primary means of working in the world.* Christians believe, and the Bible teaches, that God is sovereign. This means that God is king of the universe he made (Genesis 1:1–2:3).[1] God made the world for a very specific reason, as an expression of his glory—which basically means his amazingness. He created

---

1. There is some baggage around the belief that God made everything because there are different views on exactly *how* God made everything and, as a result, how old the universe is. This is far too big a topic to be handled in a footnote, so let me encourage you to check out some excellent (if slightly more academic) resources that interact with the different perspectives, such as Peter J. Rasor II and Theodore J. Cabal, *Controversy of the Ages: Why Christians Should Not Divide Over the Age of the Earth* (Bellingham, WA: Lexham Press, 2017), and Ken Ham, Hugh Ross, Deborah B. Haarsma, and Stephen C. Meyer, *Four Views on Creation, Evolution, and Intelligent Design* (Grand Rapids: Zondervan Academic, 2015). Regardless of the viewpoint on how he made it, the fact remains that God, as the maker of the universe, is its king.

us to enjoy and experience his amazingness, and really, to enjoy him.[2] As the maker of everything, he has complete authority over everything and the right to define how things work: gravity, quantum physics, time, light and heat, music, and so forth. Everything you can think of works the way it does because of the way he designed it, and we can understand how all these things work because God made them *to* be understood and ultimately help us to enjoy him all the more. (Also, feel free to call shenanigans on anyone who tries to say science and religion are in conflict.)

That we are all meant by design to enjoy God points us to another important truth: God is *actively* involved in the world. Despite what some say, God is not an absentee landlord or a watchmaker who wound up the gears and left us to our own devices. Christians do not believe that God is distant from us, nor do we believe he ignores what is happening in the world. He cares about us, and he cares about what happens in this world today. So he is at work actively guiding everything toward the end he has in mind: a new heaven and earth where sin, suffering, and sadness are no more because of Jesus's death and resurrection, and where God will live with his people forever (Revelation 21–22). Ultimately, this means that there's nothing—the good, the bad, *The Bachelor*—that happens in the world that doesn't somehow ultimately serve to drive us to that end (Genesis 50:20). How that works and how he uses the often-horrendous evils we see every day, we don't understand. It is a mystery, but despite

---

2. One of my favorite statements about the reason we exist comes from a nearly four-hundred-year-old document called the Westminster Shorter Catechism (a catechism is basically a curriculum but in Q&A format). The first question and answer is, "What is the chief end of man? Man's chief end is to glorify God and enjoy Him forever." A pastor named John Piper took this one step further by saying—I think accurately—that we glorify God *by* enjoying him.

being a mystery, we trust in his goodness, power, and care for us based on what we know of him.

But if God is in control, is actively involved in the world, and made everything to work in a certain way, a natural question to ask is, "Why pray at all?" Surely he doesn't need us to pray for things, right? But it's precisely because of this that we *should* pray. God *is* in control of everything, which means that he controls both the ends and the means—he knows what he is working toward, and he has determined how it will come about. Our prayers are key to that. He wants us to pray, to ask him for help, for comfort, for provision, to intervene, for miracles, and everything else we can think of because he wants us to be involved in what he is doing (Philippians 4:6–7).

WHAT SHOULD YOU PRAY ABOUT?

Practically, you can pray about anything and everything. For real. No subject is taboo. Nothing is off limits. Whatever is on your mind, whatever you want to say to God, go for it! Pray about the big things in life like jobs, relationships, how you can serve him faithfully where you are. Pray about the major decisions. But don't forget that God doesn't just care about the big things, but the little ones too. God cares about the big picture of our lives, but he also cares about the details, just as he does the birds and the wildflowers (Matthew 6:26–30). He cares as much about you finding your car keys as he does about holding all the atoms of the universe together as he does the salvation of a single person. "Our God is the God of the universe. And he is the God of square inches."[3]

3. Jared C. Wilson, *The Storytelling God: Seeing the Glory of Jesus in His Parables* (Wheaton, IL: Crossway, 2014), 66.

And if that's true, then we can pray like it's true. We can pray about things that seem too silly to pray about, and he will listen. He knows of these needs before we can even ask, and he delights in our asking.

PRACTICAL PRACTICES FOR
A HEALTHY PRAYER LIFE

It took a while to get to this perspective on prayer. Before becoming a Christian, prayer wasn't a part of my life at all because faith wasn't part of my life at all. (I mean, if there was no God—or, more accurately, if I didn't care whether there was a God—why pray?) But when I became a Christian, it became something I both wanted to do and knew I was supposed to do. The problem was that I got a lot of questionable advice about prayer from people in my church who encouraged me to pray about "expanding territories," declaring that God would or would not do, and asking for specific spiritual gifts. (I'll get to a story about that in the next chapter.)

Despite this, I fumbled my way through figuring out how to pray. I read books and blogs that talked about different prayer techniques. I tried praying at different times and in different rooms of my house. I worried (and, if I'm being honest, still do worry) about praying on autopilot—the prayers you say without thinking about what you're saying, praying more out of obligation than desire. I wondered whether I annoyed God with too many (in my opinion) inane requests or whether I was being disrespectful when I fell asleep mid-prayer at night.

As you can see, I've got a bit of baggage.

But if prayer is talking to God, *and* we believe God hears and answers our prayers, *and* we believe that there is nothing that we can't pray about, then there isn't really such a thing as a *right* or *wrong* way to pray. More specifically, there aren't a prescribed set of techniques or even prayers that we *must* use, nor are there many rules to prayer. Truthfully, outlining a long list of rules doesn't really help; for new Christians, it can be overwhelming, especially those who have no real concept of prayer at all. For more established Christians, it comes across as essentially, "Pray harder." So what I want to do instead is share with you some of the practices that I've found helpful at different times over the last sixteen years, all of which continue to play a role in how I pray today.

Prioritize prayer. We all prioritize what's important, and prayer is unquestionably among the most important things we can do. In fact, Martin Luther, a pastor and theologian who was a leader of the Protestant Reformation in the sixteenth century, cautioned Christians against not prioritizing prayer.

> Guard yourself carefully against those false, deluding ideas which tell you, "Wait a little while. I will pray in an hour; first I must attend to this or that." Such thoughts get you away from prayer into other affairs which so hold your attention and involve you that nothing comes of prayer for that day.[4]

So how do you do that? First, a great way to prioritize prayer is by scheduling it into your day, even if it's only a few minutes in the morning, another few around your lunch time, and then again at the end of your day. Second, pray in the moment. When a need comes to mind, or when anyone asks for prayer, don't wait and risk forgetting to actually do it. Instead, stop and do it right away. "Why don't we pray right now?" is a great question to ask, one that's positively biblical even, since we are encouraged

---

4. Martin Luther, "A Simple Way to Pray," in *Luther's Works*, vol. 43, *Devotional Writings II*, ed. Jaroslav Jan Pelikan, Hilton C. Oswald, and Helmut T. Lehmann (Philadelphia: Fortress, 1999), 193.

to pray continually or without ceasing (1 Thessalonians 5:17). If Christians believe God answers and works through our prayers (and we do), then that belief ought to shape our whole lives. If we believe God answers, then we ought to pray.

Pray when you feel like it. By "feel like it," I don't mean your desire but a sense of prompting. You feel like you should be praying about a specific issue, for a specific person, even something that you can't quite describe. As a general rule, if you have a sense that you should be praying, then it's a good idea to be doing so (that feeling is almost certainly being given to you by the Holy Spirit).

Pray like you talk. Virtually all churches, denominations, and individual Christians have different types of baggage when it comes to prayer. Some of us are carrying a messenger bag; others are dragging an entire luggage set. Depending on what stream of Christianity you find yourself in, you're going to pick up more along the way:

- You might find yourself in a tradition that encourages using prescribed, prewritten prayers on a regular basis.

- You may be in a tradition where people pray with language that is unintelligible to you, with fellow believers using language that is downright Shakespearean on one end of the spectrum ("Thee," "Thy," "Thou," and the like), or full of what is sometimes called Christianese on the other ("Lord, we pray for a hedge of protection by the blood of Jesus ...").

- You might also be overwhelmed with filler words (otherwise known as the "Just ... Father God, I just ..." formula).

If you haven't seen any of these things, just wait. You will (but try not to giggle when it happens; it's impolite). But if prayer is talking to God, then don't try to speak like someone else; don't try to mimic or copy the inflections and cadence of someone else. Just be *you*, whether you stutter, stumble, stammer, or, occasionally, swear. As an aside, you should know that swearing is a bit contentious among Christians. The Bible encourages restraint with our words and the "putting away" of filthy language (Colossians 3:8). The word translated "filthy" can mean abusive language or obscene and profane language. However, it should be noted that what counts as "filthy" or "profane" speech is somewhat fluid and contextual (that is, a word may or may not be considered obscene depending on your culture). That said, I'm not advocating for cursing a blue streak on a daily basis. Instead, remember that God is the creator of the universe. He made you; he made language. While language is not immune to the effects of sin, God also inspired the psalms to be written and preserved them, and they include some pretty (contextually) salty language at times.

All that to say, God can handle you unloading your frustrations in the right context. God wants to hear from *you*, not you trying to be someone you're not.

Write down your prayers. Sometimes it's helpful to write down what you're trying to say in prayer, especially if you struggle with speaking. Think of it like writing a letter to God. The advantage of this approach is that you have a record of what you've prayed that you can look back on to see how God has answered.

Pray through the Bible. While some Christian traditions encourage praying specific prayers recorded in the Bible, another approach is to pray through passages. This is a technique I learned from Donald Whitney, a seminary professor who wrote a wonderful little book called *Praying the Bible*. Here's how it works:

- Pick a passage, most likely a psalm (Psalm 8 is a good one to start with).

- Read each line slowly and pray about whatever comes to mind as you read the words.

- If your mind wanders, pray about whatever it starts wandering toward and then go back to the passage.

- Keep doing this until you run out of passage or you run out of time.[5]

Pray along with different guides. While there aren't universally prescribed prayers within the Christian faith, it can be helpful to be guided by the prayers of others. Books like the *Book of Common Prayer* (which is a collection of prayers and forms of worship services from the Anglican tradition), classic and modern devotional resources such as *Morning and Evening* (a collection of reflections by Charles Haddon Spurgeon, a prominent preacher from nineteenth-century England whose influence remains strong among Christians to this day), *The Valley of Vision* (an anonymous collection of prayers from the Puritans, a tradition that rose to prominence in seventeenth-century England and colonial America), and *Every Moment Holy* (a collection of two hundred prayers and liturgies that speak to the ordinary moments of life by Douglas McKelvey) can all add a richness to your prayer life, especially in those times when you struggle with finding words of your own.

5. Donald S. Whitney, *Praying the Bible* (Wheaton, IL: Crossway, 2015), 33.

Those are a few of the practices I've found helpful over the years; hopefully you'll find them to be as well. But there's something else you need to know about—the place of passion in prayer.

PRAYER'S PASSION

There's a lot of silly and downright harmful advice out there when it comes to prayer and passion, and it usually has to do with mistaking the outward appearance of prayer for the reality of it. For example, there was once a (thankfully now former) pastor who wrote a terrible book on what a God-focused church looked like. When he described his vision of a praying church, one that has a passionate and unyielding belief that God acts through our prayers, it was essentially the extrovert ideal on steroids—if you weren't praying on your knees, in a puddle of tears, and wailing aloud for all to hear, then could you really be a church that believes in the power of prayer?

Reading it, I couldn't help but think of a parable Jesus told. In it, Jesus describes two men going to the temple to pray. The first is a Pharisee, a member of a very pious and elite sect of the Jews in that day. He is also a braggart who uses his prayer as an opportunity to boast of how faithful he is—how much he gives, how often he fasts, and so forth. His prayer is magnificently arrogant: "God, thank you that I am not like other people" (Luke 18:11). The other man is a tax collector, a man who is hated because he makes his living overtaxing his fellow Jews in service to the Roman Empire! He is a broken man, weighed down by his own sinfulness, and can only turn to God and cry out, "God, have mercy on me, a sinner" (18:13). It is this man Jesus commends; this tax collector, with nothing to boast in whatsoever, is the one Jesus calls justified—the humble man is exalted by Jesus, while the braggart is condemned.

It's easy for us to look at the form of prayer as what defines passion. But in the Pharisee's case, the only true passion he displays is for himself; he thinks he is a pretty big deal and wants to make sure everyone, including *God*, knows it. The tax collector is the one who shows us what truly passionate prayer looks like. That passion has little to do with outward forms of prayer and everything to do with a passionate belief in the One to whom we pray. If you're more outwardly expressive, passionate prayer may look like being on your knees, in tears, and crying. But especially if you're more on the reserved side, it also might not. The point is not what you look like, the urgency of your words, or the passion in your voice. As Robert Murray M'Cheyne wrote, "Urgency in prayer does not so much consist in vehement pleading as in vehement believing. He that believes most the love and power of Jesus will obtain most in prayer."[6]

I'm not saying you should just believe harder. Instead, I want to encourage those of us who often feel weak in prayer to focus less on our ability to outwardly display our thoughts, desires, and emotions. The form of our prayer is not the measure of its faithfulness. Instead, in prayer we keep our eyes on the One who gave everything for us—Jesus, "the pioneer and perfecter of our faith" (Hebrews 12:2). Jesus is greater than our ability to express ourselves. He is what matters most in everything, including in our prayers.

6. Robert Murray M'Cheyne, *The Works of the Late Rev. Robert Murray McCheyne* (New York: Robert Carter, 1848), 1:398.

4

SHOULD I STAY OR SHOULD I GO?

//

WHAT TO LOOK FOR IN A LOCAL CHURCH

Why are these benches so close together? My knees are killing me!

It was Sunday at 10 a.m. Emily and I were sitting next to each other, and my knees were feeling like they were about to break through the back of the bench in front of me.[1] Up front, a few people took to the stage—the band—and the music began. It was the sort of innocuous pop-rock that didn't appeal to me, but people in the audience seemed to dig it.

Words appeared on the screen—the lyrics to the song—and the audience began singing. Some people put their hands in the air as they sang about how they could sing about "your" love forever and blessing "your" name.

The chorus repeated. Then it repeated again. And again. And *again*.

---

1. I did not yet know these benches were called pews. You may have never seen one before either. Few modern churches have these anymore.

Eventually, the band's leader stopped repeating the chorus, and after some somber stage patter, a middle-aged man with frosted tips, wearing jeans and an untucked party-animal shirt, took the stage. He talked for about twenty-five or thirty minutes about God's wonderful plan for our lives (or something; I wasn't listening very closely). There were notes on the screen that people were writing down on the little piece of paper they gave us at the door. A video clip—maybe from *Braveheart*—played. The lights got a bit darker. One of the band members came back on stage and started to play a chord on the keyboard while frosted-tips guy kept talking. The rest of the band came back on stage to play some more songs. Another chorus repeated, over and over again. The band leader offered a bit more patter over a soft chord, and then we were dismissed.

People didn't leave. They stuck around to hang out and talk. A few even talked to us. Then it was all over, and we made our way out to do whatever else we had planned for our day.

That was my first time going to church. Why was I there? I don't know. I didn't know whether God was really real at that point, and I still wasn't sure whether I cared. So why did I go? Because my friend Adam asked us, and Emily wanted to go.

As far as first church experiences go, it was fine, but we weren't back the next week. In fact, we didn't go back until about a month later, on the first Sunday after we were Christians. Since this was the only church we knew and our friend already went there, we went too. It was good for us. We made a few friends. Emily and I got married there. I started volunteering in the kids' program and in other areas. I even went on my first overseas ministry trip with this church. Was it perfect? Of course not. But it was genuinely where we needed to be for our first two or three years as Christians.

The problem is that we were there for a little more than four.

What happened about halfway through? We'll get there. But first, let's back up a bit and ask, *Why be a part of a church at all?*

WHAT IS A CHURCH?

Being a part of a local church, just like reading the Bible and prayer, is critical to your life as a Christian. It's the third leg of a stool that must be present if we're not going to fall on our tails. We need to be fully known and fully know other people—to be a part of a community where we can actually grow in our faith. But it's also, arguably, the most challenging of the three. Why? Because Christians are *people.*

Many Christians are incredibly kind and considerate, but all of us have the same big problem as all other people: we all sin.[2] We all still have times when we put ourselves ahead of others, still act in a way that made sense before Jesus saved us. Old habits and all that. Because people are people, it means that we inevitably are going to annoy, frustrate, hurt, and disappoint one another. Being a Christian doesn't suddenly mean that we are perfect. Far from it. Christians—no matter how mature, no matter their background and upbringing—are all a bunch of hot messes working out their crap together with God's and one another's help.

That's really important when we try to understand what the church—and more specifically, a local church—*is.* A church, in its most basic sense, is a group of people committed to worshiping Jesus together and seeking the good of one another, their

---

2. Note that I didn't say that we're all sinners. Because of Jesus's death and resurrection, the identity of sinner—a person who lives in rebellion against God's goodness and rule over the universe—doesn't really apply to people who believe in Jesus. When we sin, we are acting against our nature, being who and what we are not, rather than embracing our true nature.

communities, and the world. While they might look different in terms of its systems and structures—how leaders are identified and how they choose to order our worship gatherings may look different from one church and one tradition to the next—all healthy churches should be able to identify with this description.

SEVEN SIGNS OF A HEALTHY CHURCH

So what does a church that worships Jesus really look like? Before we get into the specifics, you need to know something about worship. Worship means "to ascribe worth." It is to think, speak, and act in a way that says that we believe someone or something is more important—or even more valuable—than ourselves. As Christians, that someone is God in all his three-in-oneness.[3] How we handle money, the way we work, how we use our time, and everything else we do is an act of worship, a way of saying that God—that Jesus—is more valuable to us than anything else.

Within the context of a church community, both when we gather to worship Jesus and when we are apart, it looks something like this:

Jesus is the focus. While this *should* be a given, it isn't. Politics, culture warring, and other forms of cultural appropriation (taking the values of the culture and equating them with biblical truth) constantly threaten to distract the church from Jesus and the gospel. This is true everywhere in every culture and in all contexts. Christians living in North America may be inclined to put personal and collective wealth forward as a sign of God's favor or to overly emphasize numbers (baptisms and butts in seats) as proof that God is at work. Sometimes that's true, but

3. Because the words that are most frequently translated as worship mean "to bow down or kneel," it's helpful to think of worship as a reverential deference, a way of saying with all of our being that God is greater than us.

not always. One healthy church may struggle to pay its bills while another is flush with cash. A healthy church may be bursting at the seams while another sees sixty people on a good Sunday. Churches tend to put more stock in these measurements because they're visible; they're easy to measure. And while they matter, when they become our focus, we begin to major in the minors. A healthy church recognizes that growth belongs to the Lord and that the primary aim is to be intensely focused on Jesus in the best ways possible:

- They sing songs that remind you of the beauty of the gospel, and of God's nature, his character, and his promises that belong to you because of Jesus's death and resurrection.[4]

- They preach sermons that draw attention to the gospel from every passage of the Bible (Luke 24:27; John 5:39; 17:3; 20:30–31).

- They baptize people as a declaration that they belong to Jesus, that their sins have died with him, and that they have received the promise of new life given through his resurrection (Matthew 28:19).[5]

- They take Communion, or the Lord's Supper, to remind us of Jesus's death for our sins—the bread

---

4. Many more established Christians will equate this aspect of worship—music—with its totality. Worship includes singing and is not less than singing, but it is more than singing.

5. There are two main views of baptism within Christian communities. Some Christians believe that we should baptize people as infants (assuming they have believing parents), signifying that they are members of the covenant community. This view has been the dominant one throughout the majority of Christianity's two thousand years, but the Bible does not offer much by way of support for it that I've seen. Other Christians believe that people should be baptized only after they have made a profession of faith. I hold to this latter view because I believe that it is what we see modeled in Scripture and that it is the most well-supported from the Bible itself.

symbolizing his body that was broken for us, and the wine or juice (depending on what tradition you find yourself in) representing his blood that was shed for us (1 Corinthians 11:17–26).

If Jesus isn't at the center, a group of people may be many things—they may even call themselves a church—but a local church they are not.

Character is prioritized over skill. It's easy to be enamored with the skills and abilities of leaders, especially when it comes to teaching. But the Bible doesn't do that; instead, without saying that teaching ability is unimportant it focuses on something radically different: character. Christian leaders are to be "above reproach" (1 Timothy 3:2), which means they're to have stellar character, to the point that no one could bring any legitimate charge forward about them. And while there is more to say about leaders (and I will in a couple chapters), this is to be the most important thing about them. A person might be able to teach, be a great visionary, or highly administrative, but if that person is narcissistic, a lover of money, prone to outbursts of anger, arrogant, quarrelsome, or pugnacious, they have no business leading any part of a church.

The Bible is the standard. The Bible is the norming norm, meaning it is the measurement by which we evaluate our words, thoughts, and deeds. We are taught by it, encouraged by it, and corrected by it. (2 Timothy 3:16–17). Without the Bible, all we have are opinions—and given how often our opinions change, that is terrifying, isn't it?[6]

---

6. That is not to say that everyone reads and understand the Bible the same. Some passages are harder to understand than others. Genuine Christians interpret several passages differently, too. But even when there is a difference in interpretation, it's usually true that all involved in the disagreement would believe that the Bible itself is true. (If there is error, the error is on their part.)

People are known. A healthy church is one where the people are involved in one another's lives. They take the time needed and provide the safety required for people—especially those who are dealing with a lot of junk—to open up. They experience the truth that when one of us suffers, we all suffer, and when one of us is honored, we all rejoice alongside that one (1 Corinthians 12:26).

Sin is taken seriously. A healthy church culture deals with sin in a way that reflects the gospel. This means we hold one another—leaders and congregation members alike—accountable for our actions, and when we sin against one another, church discipline is practiced consistently, often with tears. It's not a cult-y kind of shunning culture that expects everyone to toe the party line or align themselves under a specific leader. It's one that encourages Christians to be who they are by pursuing a holy life, a life of joy in and faithfulness to Jesus because Jesus saved them from their sins (Matthew 18:15–20; 1 Corinthians 5:1–13; Jude 22).

Non-Christians are loved. We want to help non-Christians believe in Jesus, so we share the gospel with them. We want them to understand what we believe. We want them to build relationships with Christians and see how we live. We want them to have the freedom to ask any question—and I really do mean *any* question—about the faith that they want. But we also want to protect them from participating in ways that they're not meant to. So yeah, invite non-Christians to come with you to church. Ask them to come hang out with other Christians. But non-Christians shouldn't be encouraged to take part in the actual ministry of the church—things like volunteering in a kids' ministry or playing music or anything like that. It's wrong to do this because these are all acts of worship. People serve in kids' ministry (or they should) because they love Jesus and want kids to know Jesus too. People sing and play music because they want to play that music for Jesus. So to ask someone who doesn't worship Jesus to do things that are all about worshiping Jesus wouldn't be right.

Compassion is a way of life. From literally the beginning of the church, compassion and care for those in need has been a defining characteristic of the Christian life. The early believers shared all they had with one another, to the degree that "there was no one needy among them" (Acts 4:34, NET). Christians, historically, have been at the forefront of orphan care and adoption efforts, providing healthcare to anyone and everyone in need, the abolition of slavery, education movements, and so many more. Christianity was radical in its early days because women were treated with the same dignity and respect as men. Christians rejected abortion and infanticide, instead opting to provide homes for unwanted children, or those deemed as having less value (which usually meant girls in male-oriented societies). Where churches were built, hospitals and schools followed.[7] Christians' commitment to compassionate care in our earliest days was so powerful that it put the surrounding culture—and its leaders to shame. A healthy church today carries on that tradition. It makes the most of every opportunity to care for those in need in the church, the community, and the world. How this looks may differ from church-to-church and community-to-community: For example, some run adoption and pregnancy care ministries. Others maintain food and clothing pantries, providing needed goods for little or no cost. Others maintain a benevolence fund to provide financially for urgent needs. But all do it as an act of worship, demonstrating our love for God in our love for others (Matthew 22:39).[8]

7. The First Council of Nicaea, one of the earliest gatherings of church leaders from all over the known world, declared that wherever a church or cathedral was built, a hospital would be as well.

8. For a thorough treatment on this subject, I would, again, encourage reading my book, *Awaiting a Savior: The Gospel, the New Creation, and the End of Poverty* (Minneapolis: Cruciform Press, 2011).

Let's be honest, though: there isn't a single church that is going to perfectly reflect any of these signs of a healthy church. No church can; after all, people are involved. You know what you're like. I know what I'm like, too. Anyone looking at a church for perfection is going to be more disappointed than someone hoping that a good story will come from whatever movie Nicolas Cage is starring in this week. It's possible, but not likely.

We can't worry about perfection, but we should expect consistency. It all starts with the first two signs in the list above: if a church is focused on Jesus and if it is led by people of character, the rest will follow.

SLOWLY (BUT QUICKLY) MOVING APART

Our first church was probably the best place for us to be as brand-new Christians. The leaders gave us lots of space and encouragement to work out the issues we faced coming into the faith. They made us feel welcome. They made us feel like family. But it wasn't too long—maybe a year or so after we became Christians—that I started to see where we were already beginning to go in different directions, especially as I started to develop convictions around important (and sometimes less important) areas of the Christian life. One difference that started to come up was what we believed about spiritual gifts and one gift in particular: speaking in tongues.

Christians of virtually every tradition agree that the Holy Spirit gives believers gifts and abilities for the purpose of carrying the gospel forward and building up the church. Some of these gifts include teaching, encouragement, acts of service, and so forth. Where different Christian traditions disagree is over whether the miraculous sign gifts described in the Gospels and Acts—people prophesying (speaking a message from the Lord), healing the sick, speaking in unknown languages, and the like—will be experienced today. My first church was part of a denomination that believed that we should experience these gifts today and that if the Holy Spirit is present in a Christian's life, the primary evidence will be that they speak in tongues or a previously unknown language.[9]

But as I studied the Bible as a new believer, I didn't read any passage that suggested that this specific gift, let alone any one gift, was something every Christian should expect to experience. Instead, I saw Paul argue forcefully for the opposite in 1 Corinthians 12–14. There he says the evidence of the Holy Spirit's presence and work in a Christian's life is not that someone speaks in an unknown language, but love: "If I speak human or angelic tongues but do not have love, I am a noisy gong or a clanging cymbal" (1 Corinthians 13:1). Love—love that is patient, kind, that does not seek its own way, but seeks to build up others—that is the evidence that the Holy Spirit is with us and should be our greatest concern (1 Corinthians 13:4–6).

So I started asking questions of a longtime member of the church who had taken me under his wing. I explained to him what I was (and was not) seeing. We disagreed and kept disagreeing. He prayed that I would experience this gift. I prayed that I would too, if it was the Lord's will. I felt a massive amount of anxiety about it. After all, if I didn't have this gift, was I even a Christian at all? Finally, one evening as I drove home from this man's house, I began to pray what was probably the least godly prayer I've prayed as a believer: "Lord, if you want me to experience this gift, could you please make it happen so I can get it over with already?"

And clear as day, in a way that I had never experienced before or since, I received an answer—not exactly an audible voice, but

9. This belief is drawn from the events shown in Acts 2:4; 10:46; and 19:6.

a voice nonetheless. "No, that is not what I have for you. Don't ask again."

Immediately, I felt a weight lift. Whatever self-imposed burden I felt from the expectation to speak in tongues was gone, never to return. Leaders in the church kept praying that I would, but I never did. I didn't need to.

GOOD (AND BAD) REASONS TO
LEAVE A LOCAL CHURCH

While this wasn't the reason that Emily and I ultimately left the church, it played a role. It was the first step in a much longer process. Staying or leaving at a church usually isn't decided over one thing. It's figured out over time and with many different factors coming into play. However, not all reasons for leaving a church are created equal. Some of them are wise, and others, not so much. Here are some bad reasons to leave a church:

1. **The music.** You may have strong opinions about music. Whether it's because a church does or doesn't sing hymns, the band of amateur volunteers isn't as good as the band that recorded the songs, or the band sings the same chorus thirty-seven thousand times over, frustration over this is rarely, if ever, a good reason to start looking for a new church.

2. **Preaching style.** When people leave a church over the preaching, it usually isn't about the content. Usually it's about style—the simple fact that the majority of pastors don't sound as professional as some of the ones we listen to on podcasts. But if our pastors were really slick communicators, they wouldn't be our pastors.

3. **Coffee or other amenities.** Some people get frustrated about a church not offering coffee or other amenities. As a general rule, church coffee is trash, which is what happens when you use one tablespoon of fourteen-year-old grounds for every twelve gallons of water. On the scale of drinkable coffee, it's the one type that is less drinkable than Tim Hortons or Dunkin' Donuts.[10] So don't expect it to be good, and don't be disappointed if it's not there. The same goes with other kinds of amenities, whether it's on-site bookstores and libraries (where the issue is what is or is not available), gymnasiums and classrooms, pews or chairs, intricate lighting set-ups, and more. Some people want all the bells and whistles, while others want to keep things as basic as possible.

4. **Boredom.** Sometimes people leave for reasons that are slightly more ambiguous. They might say, "I'm not being fed," or, "I feel like God is calling us somewhere else, but I don't know where." They may even point to ministry programs that aren't present in the church. While there are times when these may be legitimately true, often they're used as a cover for something else—that they're no longer satisfied with the way the church they're currently a part of does things and want to see whether the grass is greener elsewhere. They're probably going to be disappointed.

---

10. Tim Hortons is a Canadian coffee and donut chain whose coffee tastes like resignation, disappointment, and menthol cigarettes. Dunkin' Donuts' coffee takes like lukewarm brown, which makes it slightly more palatable.

None of these reasons are good reasons to leave a church. In fact, all of them are symptoms of one greater issue: that people place a greater value on their personal preferences than the church as a whole. This is foolish. Actually, foolish doesn't go far enough. Putting our personal preferences ahead of the church, putting ourselves ahead of others, is wrong. It's a mindset that is opposed to the gospel on a very practical level, since we are called to "consider others more important than" ourselves—the same attitude that took Jesus to the cross for us (Philippians 2:4–11). But even though there are a lot of dumb reasons to leave a church, some truly are wise. Here are just a handful:

1. **Moving.** Whether you're going to a new city or a new country, moving is a good reason to join a new church.

2. **Unaddressed sin.** When sin is left unaddressed, or swept under the rug, you don't have a church. I don't know what you have, but it's not a church. This includes gossip, slander, sexual abuse and sexual immorality of all sorts, greed, and other forms of idolatry, which is to functionally worship anything that isn't God.[11] If any of these are diminished, brushed off, or otherwise ignored, you need to get away fast.

3. **Pastoral failure.** The Bible often describes pastoral ministry in agricultural terms, particularly in the language of shepherding. Pastors are to care for the

---

11. In the Bible, idolatry is usually described in a literal sense—worshiping false gods (whether imaginary or actual demonic beings) or statues that look like created beings (animals, people, etc.). But idolatry includes money, sex, family, status, and just about anything else you can imagine. A really helpful and accessible book on the subject of idolatry is Timothy Keller, *Counterfeit Gods: The Empty Promises of Money, Sex, and Power, and the Only Hope That Matters* (New York: Penguin Books, 2011).

people of the church like a shepherd cares for his flock: feeding them, meeting their needs, tending their wounds, and protecting them from danger. But sometimes, churches, especially those that are in regions where Christianity haunts the air like cigarette tar clings to wallpaper, put a greater emphasis on people being self-sustaining as disciples than on being cared for as people. We're told we need to learn to feed ourselves (which is not untrue), but we're not always shown how. Especially in the early days of your faith, you need church leaders who will show you how to read the Bible, how to discern between sound and false teaching, and how to oppose heresy in a way that reflects God's character. If a church's leaders aren't willing to help this happen, then it's probably wise to find leaders who will.

4. **False teaching.** Christians tend to divide our beliefs into different categories. There are certain beliefs that we consider *primary*, or of first importance. They're the things that we believe because if we don't, we can't really call ourselves Christian in any meaningful way. There are other beliefs that you might hear described as *secondary* matters. These are important beliefs that shape our expression of our faith but are not faith defining. How to address societal issues such as racism, the church's role in caring for the poor, and the limiting of certain roles in the church are a few of these. These secondary matters are where most disagreements between Christians exist, and with rare exception, we can agree to disagree and still be part of one local church. But disagreements over primary, faith-defining matters are much more serious. Where there is disagreement

over matters such as God's nature, Jesus's humanity and divinity, his death and resurrection, and how salvation works, among others, we cannot agree to disagree.[12] False teaching, which is also called heresy, is not something that we can overlook. Sometimes false teaching is presented overtly—the teacher will outright teach something contrary to an essential truth of the faith. More frequently, false teaching shows up as a gospel plus message, where there is something you need to add to the good news of Jesus, such as obeying additional commands that the Bible doesn't require, or elevating secondary issues into a place of first importance. (So If someone tries to elevate a perspective on gender roles to this category, for example, run for the hills.)

But sometimes, even when genuine disagreement exists, it is difficult to know whether or when it's time to leave. It's so easy to get wrong, especially if you're not entirely certain if you've got a good reason to leave. Can you or should you leave a church where you agree on the big issues, but have some serious disagreements on secondary ones? Maybe. In some rare cases, probably. But leaving is a big deal, something that shouldn't be done lightly. Instead, as much as possible, our default inclination should be to stay. If the gospel is genuinely being proclaimed, sin is not being ignored, disagreements are not compromising our consciences, and the tensions that exist are not causing us to

---

12. In addition to his existence as three-in-one (the Trinity), God's eternal existence, his complete and exhaustive knowledge of all things (omniscience), his inexhaustible power (omnipotence), his ever-presentness (omnipresence), and his active and intimate engagement with the world he made (immanence) and distinction from that world (transcendence) are all essential to what we believe about God. If we reject these, we redefine God into something other than himself.

sin against others, I would encourage staying. That's why some people will feel compelled to stay in a situation where another might leave, even in the midst of serious disagreement, because that specific local church or the denomination it is a part of is home. They genuinely love it and want to be a part of it. Perhaps they'll be able to stay and thrive. But for others, there is a clear moment when God prompts them to leave, where either they see that staying will not be good for them, a boundary is crossed in a specific area, or (in some cases) there is an irrepressible sense that it's time to go, even if it's not clear why.[13] And when God prompts, it is unwise to ignore. I learned that the hard way.

WHEN I KNEW IT WAS TIME TO GO
(AND WHAT HAPPENED WHEN
I DIDN'T SOON ENOUGH)

In fall 2008, Emily and I took a walk one Sunday morning, our eighteen-month-old daughter in tow. We were chitchatting about the regular stuff of life, when out of nowhere I said, "We're not going to be at our church forever. I don't know when we'll leave but eventually, we're going to." She thought for a moment and agreed, and we carried on with our conversation. A couple of weeks later, we were at church, and the associate pastor was preaching. There was a fire in his words as he spoke of the call to be sent into the world to spread the gospel. Toward the end of the message, he said words that burned in my soul:

---

13. There's a helpful conversation about this issue on *The Russell Moore Show* that explores the experiences of two Christian leaders' experience with leaving the denomination they were raised in after years of high-profile service within it as Bible teachers and leading different organizations. You can listen to that conversation: "Beth Moore Didn't Expect Us to Be Us: Lessons in Leaving and Staying," *The Russell Moore Show*, episode 1, October 6, 2021, https://www.christianitytoday.com/ct/podcasts/russell-moore-show/russell-moore-and-beth-moore-live-in-nashville.html.

"Some of you in this room right now need to ask to be sent out."

Something inside me started nagging. "Ask to be sent out. Ask. *Now*."

I did not ask. It was one of the biggest mistakes I made as a new-ish Christian. If I had, I would have saved myself—and them—a great deal of frustration. Within weeks of that Sunday, I became one of the more persnickety and kind of jerky church-goers you ever did see. I'd go on Sunday, listen to the message, make notes, and vent about everything that I heard that was wrong on the way home. I constantly felt anxious about even going and was eager to skip, which is not how I wanted to live, both for my own sake and for my growing family's. We started part-time attending another church closer to home while our car was broken. We didn't join because its pastor started overtly preaching heresy. (I later learned he had been subtly doing so for some time.) When our car was repaired, we went back to church, but it was too much for me. I was done.

I told the pastor we were going to leave. It was a polite meeting, but I could tell right away that he was hurt that we were leaving. After all, he had baptized Emily and me. He performed our wedding. He counseled us through those tumultuous first months as believers. He was a good pastor for us—and the church *is* a good church that wants people to know Jesus and are using many means to do it. But after those first couple of years, it wasn't the right church for *me* and my family. But I waited too long to realize that. And because I waited too long, our leaving was marked more by a broken relationship, one that my delay had caused. Maybe if I had obeyed the prompting I felt that Sunday in 2008, things might have been different. Perhaps I would have stories of how grateful I am that they encouraged me to obey what I was sensing from the Lord. Instead, I have my conviction that I was still right to leave, but completed with my regrets over how it went down.

When the Spirit prompts you to go, and it's undeniable, obey. Do it with open, honest communication, with input from others, and with a great deal of prayer, but obey. If you don't, you'll probably find yourself with a list of regrets similar to mine.

FINDING YOUR FIT IN A HEALTHY CHURCH

By now, I hope you've already found a great, healthy church filled with people who love Jesus and love you. It's also possible that you're still trying to find where you fit. Whether you're already in a great church or you're still trying to find one where you belong, here's what I would encourage:

Pray for wisdom. God wants you to be in community with other Christians. For real. He will even help you find the place where he wants you. So ask him as you explore. He will answer, giving you wisdom to see where the right place is and discernment to recognize places that may be unhealthy for you too.

Take your time. You might find a great church right away, but you also might not. And that's okay. It can take time to build relationships and for a church community to begin to feel like a family.

Focus on direction, not perfection. No church is perfect. Even if you love the one you've found, it's going to be messy in some areas, and it will fall short of its own expectations. (Remember, people are involved. But if you can see that the church is helping people to know and love Jesus more and is showing the world a little something of what he is like, then it's probably a solid place to be.

Choose a place you can invest in. Being a part of a healthy Christian community means being involved and invested. As you look for a church to call home, even as you think about how it might help you, consider how you can be a gift to that community as well.

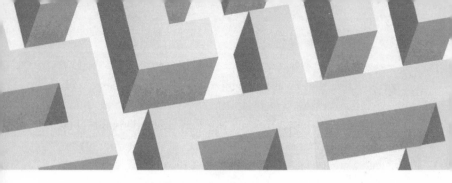

5

IT'S A BEAUTIFUL WORLD

//

YOU DON'T HAVE TO GIVE UP EVERYTHING
YOU LIKE WHEN YOU BECOME A CHRISTIAN

I was five years old when I read the story that made me fall in love with comics. I was at a babysitter's house and was put in front of a banana box full of comic books and magazines. "Go ahead and read whatever you want," the sitter said. As I rummaged through the box, I found one that intrigued me, its cover long ago torn away and discarded: "What if Conan the Barbarian Walked the Earth Today?"[1] The premise was that, while on a quest in the (fictional) Hyborian Age, Conan was transported from ancient Cimmeria to 1970s New York City. Wackiness ensued, as one would expect. Conan began fighting with the police. He broke up a riot, got shot, and got intimate with a female cab driver, all before discovering how he could return to his own time—which he did, of course.

---

1. This comic book was published in 1977 by Marvel Comics, two years before I was born. It's available online if you want to Google it. Yes, I am fantastically nerdy.

Was it a good story? Probably not. Was it fun? Absolutely. That story, for all its hokeyness and clichés, opened my eyes to one fact: comic books are among the most inventive storytelling mediums, a form in which creativity can run wild. While most people might think of them as primarily being superhero fare, they have room for all genres: whether you're a fan of murder mysteries, romantic comedies, postapocalyptic horror, dystopian science fiction, day-in-the-life tales, or art house-inspired stories, you can tell them in comics. If you can come up with an interesting story, and an artist can draw it, it can become a reality.

I don't just love comic books, though. I love movies, television shows, and books of all sorts. I love modern Western mystery stories and British literature. I dig movies about midlevel bands trying to make it and books about grumpy record store owners trying to navigate early midlife crises. Walking into a bookstore, shopping online, browsing a streaming service and discovering something new—even if it's only new to *me*—is thrilling. Why? Because the act of creating—and of discovering what others have created—is thrilling.

Up to this point, we've been looking mostly at the mechanics of the Christian life, talking about different habits to develop and nurture to have a healthy relationship with God and people. But these habits are only one part of what it means to live as a Christian. A massive part of our lives is spent applying what we believe to our experiences and different aspects of our lives, both important and seemingly inconsequential. Which is where creativity—specifically music, movies, books, and pop culture in general—comes into play. When you become a Christian, what changes about what you create and what you consume? Do you have to give up everything you used to enjoy because of your faith? Do you have to stop making what you loved making because you follow Jesus?

GOD CREATED CREATIVITY

There are certain things a utilitarian worldview doesn't have a strong explanation for. Creativity—writing stories, making music, building, designing, shaping, and innovating—is at the top of that list. Why do we create works of great beauty, songs that move the soul, and stories that captivate our imaginations, none of which have a natural place in a worldview that values usefulness above all else? What is it that motivates human beings to be creative?

Fundamentally, we create because God is creative. Creativity is valuable because God does it. He made all the stuff of this universe. He made the subatomic particles that make up your body, even as he made the moon and the stars (Genesis 1:1–2:2). When he made everything, he intentionally made things beautiful, awe-inspiring, and wonderful, precisely the way a God who wants us to know and recognize his power and nature would (Romans 1:20). That includes *us*. God made us to be unique, distinct from every other creature that exists; he made us like him, capable of representing something of his nature and character to the world around us.[2] So we are relational because God is relational, eternally existing in relationship as the Father, Son, and Spirit. We are moral beings because God defines and exemplifies morality. And we are creative beings, too, enjoying and pursuing creative endeavors because he is creative. Whether that creativity is expressed in making music for all to hear, writing poems that no one will ever see, developing a software program, or finding new ways to get a toddler to eat something (anything!), creativity is tied to our very being. We can't *not* be creative because we are like our Creator.

---

2. The Bible uses the description of humanity being made "in his image" as a catchall for all of this and more besides (Genesis 1:26–27).

Human creativity shows up early in the biblical narrative. Adam, the first man, got his creativity on when he was naming the animals (Genesis 2:19), but hit his stride when he met his wife in Genesis 2:23, composing the world's first (and certainly not last) ode to a woman. Later, it was a descendant of the world's first murderer, Cain, who created instruments (Genesis 4:21), and another who developed instruments of bronze and iron (Genesis 4:22). Later still, we see that the first person described as being filled with the Holy Spirit is an artist, Bezalel, who was filled "with God's Spirit, with wisdom, understanding, and ability in every kind of craft to design artistic works in gold, silver, and bronze, to cut gemstones for mounting, and to carve wood for work in every kind of artistic craft" (Exodus 35:31–33). King David was a brilliant poet and musician as well, crafting many of the psalms that exist in our Bible today (for example, Psalms 8; 23; 51). I could go on, but the point is simple: We create because God is creative, and God calls creativity good—even if our creative efforts are sometimes decidedly *not* good.

SWIMMING IN A SEA OF MEDIOCRITY

Since God made us to be creative, I believe Christians should be leading the way in every creative field. Everything we do should be better than everything else that we see out in the marketplace and in the world. After all, everything we do is to be done to the glory of God (Galatians 3:23; 1 Corinthians 10:31). That means creativity is an act of worship, which means that it should be done to the best of our ability, both personally and collectively.

For centuries, the greatest works of art were created by Christians. Many great visual artists have been Christians, including Albrecht Dürer and Rembrandt, and much of the old masters' work draws on explicit religious themes and imagery. The world's greatest composers—including Handel, Bach, Mozart, Beethoven, and many others—wrote music that expressed their faith, as an act of worship. Many of the greatest novelists and storytellers of all time were Christians as well, including Jane Austen, J. R. R. Tolkien, Nathaniel Hawthorne, Charlotte Brontë, and William Shakespeare.

But somewhere along the way, we lost the plot. Because we succumbed to fear, laziness, or the desire to make a quick buck, many Christian artists stopped innovating and settled for mediocrity. Instead of leading, they chose to follow in the footsteps of the world at large, offering bad copies with a vaguely spiritual message inserted. "Like the Foo Fighters? Well, then try these guys who kind of sound a bit like them, but totally love Jesus!"[3]

When I first became a Christian, people I met at church encouraged me to listen to music that, instead of being about women, might have been about Jesus (but was still actually about women, I think). They would recommend novels written by Christians that usually had something to do with the end of the world (but without any significant mention of Jesus coming back). They'd show movies where the main characters' lives were spiraling down the toilet until—suddenly—one of them realized that they needed God (generally speaking), and then everything was better. There was a great deal of pressure to like things that weren't very good, simply because they were vaguely Christian in their content. I tried to listen, read, and watch with an open mind. But because most of what was recommended was garbage, I gave up and went back to listening to good music and reading great books instead.[4]

3. Much of what is popular in the culture at large is also wildly mediocre. So we have a situation where mediocrity begets more mediocrity.
4. Today I live near Nashville, Tennessee, which is where most of said garbage gets made. Many of my friends and coworkers are amazed when I tell them I don't know most of the people they listened to faithfully growing up.

Reading that, hopefully you noticed an important word: most. Even though there's a great deal of absolute trash masquerading as art that is peddled to Christians, there are many Christians who do take seriously the belief that creativity is an act of worship. Andrew Peterson, Kendrick Lamar, and Sandra McCracken write songs that reflect their faith in profound ways while being artistically excellent.[5] S. D. Smith, Leif Enger, K. B. Hoyle, N. D. Wilson, Frederick Buechner, and many others write stories that are shaped by their faith (even while their stories are not explicitly Christian). Rommel Ruiz, Jason Fabok, John Hendrix, Makoto Fujimura, and many others create incredible works of art—including comic books!—in part as an expression of their faith.

As a Christian, you do not need to be resigned to artistic mediocrity. There are Christians who make great art. There are non-Christians who make great art, too. There are Christians who make terrible art, and non-Christians who make terrible art, too. Our job is to both *make* and *enjoy* great books, movies, music, and every other creative endeavor under the sun, in a way that reflects our love of God as the One who created creativity.[6]

So what does that mean, exactly? When it comes to the act of creating as Christians, there's a helpful principle that comes from 1 Corinthians 6:12. This verse is part of a response the apostle Paul offers to questions around appropriate conduct by Christians in a city called Corinth. The Corinthian believers' question had to do with freedom: If the gospel freed them from

---

5. Peterson is one of the most underrated artists who makes music for the church. He is also an outstanding author whose four-book series *The Wingfeather Saga* nearly got him listed in this paragraph twice.
6. Once again, this points us to the purpose of humanity being to glorify God and enjoy him forever, as the Westminster Catechism puts it.

IT'S A BEAUTIFUL WORLD

the consequences and constraints of God's law—if they were free in Christ—did that mean they could do whatever they wanted? "Everything is permissible" was their mindset; nothing should be forbidden. But Paul wisely counters it by saying that "not everything is beneficial," as he helps them think more deeply about the wise use of their freedom. Freedom is only beneficial insofar as it does not lead you, or someone else, to become entrapped by or enslaved to something else.

That's the principle we need to focus on when we're talking about creating as Christians. We might feel the freedom to make whatever we desire, and to a certain extent we can. But our creative efforts do not solely belong to us; they do not exist in a vacuum. We are giving something to others in sharing our creative efforts—even if that something is primarily a glimpse into our own hearts. This means what we make should be beneficial not only to ourselves, but to others. So when we create anything, we should be doing so with a mindset focused on what is good, beautiful, and true.[7]

The goodness of creativity. To say any creative effort is good might seem squishy because we tend to look at good subjectively (the same is true for beautiful). In one sense, it's true that goodness is subjective, but that's not the only sense in which we should see the goodness of creativity. Instead, we should look at it from the perspective of value. As Christians, we should recognize that the act of creating is valuable. When we create anything,

---

7. These three virtues form the pillars of Plato's philosophical system, with these three representing aspects of ultimate reality. These virtues also permeate the entire Bible, but not in the same way as in Plato's thinking. Plato and his students saw these virtues as impersonal; they weren't truly something that could be interacted with. The Bible, on the other hand, shows that these virtues all find their source in God himself, as they are all aspects of his being. A short book that shaped a lot of my thinking on the subject of art and the Christian life is Francis Schaeffer, *Art and the Bible* (Downers Grove, IL: InterVarsity, 1973 [2006]).

whether poetry, paintings, or pottery, we are acting according to our nature. In a very real sense, all our creative efforts—even the most seemingly mundane ones—are acts of worship, even when they're not explicitly Christian in content.

The beauty of creativity. Beauty in creativity has two senses. The most common way we understand it is in the subjective sense; it is based on our experience of seeing something that we believe to be beautiful. What we like, what is pleasing to us in some way, is beautiful, even if it might not be beautiful to everyone else. But beauty is not purely subjective; it cannot be. For if beauty were purely subjective, the concept of beauty itself would be meaningless. Beauty exists in an objective sense as well, rooted in the being and properties of what is seen as beautiful. The ultimate source of that beauty is God himself, who is beautiful, and everything he does is beautiful.[8] Because God is beautiful, we want to put beautiful things into the world. We want to be excellent in what we create, whether a well-told story, a well-composed photograph, a soaring score, or a passionate performance. Everything we do should be characterized by excellence—to be, in an objective sense, beautiful—regardless of whether those interacting with it subjectively enjoy it.

8. Philosophers and theologians, from Aristotle and Plato to Augustine and Immanuel Kant, have discussed this relationship between the subjective and objective natures of beauty for thousands of years. Augustine, a fourth-century Christian theologian, shows how embracing both senses leads to worship when he writes,

    "But I, O my God and my Adornment, can even sing a hymn to Thee from this and offer up a sacrifice of praise to Him who sacrifices for me, since the beautiful designs which are transmitted through souls into artful hands come from that Beauty which is above souls, for which my soul sighs day and night."

    Augustine of Hippo, *Confessions*, ed. Roy Joseph Deferrari, trans. Vernon J. Bourke, Fathers of the Church 21 (Washington, DC: Catholic University of America Press, 1953), 310.

The truth of creativity. To call creativity true means that Christians should be unflinchingly honest in what we make. We are neither naively optimistic nor cynically pessimistic. We don't pretend that sin doesn't exist, but we also don't wallow in the muck and mire. Truth in creativity means looking at reality as it really is (even if we are making up fantastical worlds, they will only resonate with others if they contain truth about reality as they experience it). It also means that what we create is an expression of who we are. Our difficulties and joys are a part of what we create, so we shouldn't shy away from that or try to turn what we make into an evangelism tool.[9] This also means we have a tremendous amount of freedom to create.

ENJOYING CREATIVITY
THE WAY GOD INTENDED

As Christians, our creative efforts are focused on what is good, beautiful, and true. That is the kind of art within any medium that is good for the world. Like the act of creating, what we consume should be informed by these truths as well. That also means it involves exercising discernment, or judging what you're engaging with wisely, based on three factors: its quality, its content, and your season of life.

Quality counts. Our ability to enjoy virtually any creative effort is determined by its quality. When a song is poorly composed, we know it. When a book lacks a plot or is filled with hackneyed phrases and utilitarian writing, we are not unaware (even if said book sells gazillions). When a movie's special

---

9. "Christian art is the expression of the whole life of the whole person who is a Christian. What a Christian portrays in his art is the totality of life. Art is not to be solely a vehicle for some sort of self-conscious evangelism" (Schaeffer, *Art and the Bible*, Kindle loc. 573).

effects are subpar (or overused) and performances are lifeless, we notice. On the flip side, clever musical composition moves us. Engaging plots and clever sentences make books a delight to read. Thoughtful acting and wisely used effects make the experience of watching a movie a joy. In the same way as when we create anything, we need to care about quality of what we're consuming because quality matters. God is never honored by mediocrity, no matter its message or content. God made everything *good*, not simply in its morality but in quality. If we're going to enjoy creative works that glorify God, then we need to care about the quality of the creative works we enjoy.

Content counts, too. Having said that, quality isn't the sole factor in determining what is God-glorifying with entertainment and creative efforts. The message being communicated matters as much as the methods used. This doesn't mean that there is necessarily certain content that is always off-limits (although some content, such as pornography, certainly is).[10] We can't be simplistic in our approach and say that we should only watch movies with an overt spiritual message, only read books written by and for Christians, or listen exclusively to music that has some kind of vaguely spiritual message to it. This is how too many people I know who grew up in Christian families were taught to approach pop culture: secular = bad, "Christian" = good. Listening to a Muse album or reading Neil Gaiman's *The Sandman* might seem like a great idea, but it's slippery slope to apostasy (or something).

---

10. Christians should not be watching, reading, or otherwise participating in pornography because it is designed with one purpose in mind: to incite and reshape our sexual desires in ways that are contrary to the way we've been designed. More on that in the next chapter.

This does a disservice to everyone—creators and audiences, Christians and non-Christians alike—because it denies reality. Specifically, it denies the reality of sin's effects on everything and all of us. Sin is our innate desire to do, think, or say anything that displeases God. Even after we become Christians, we keep sinning, even though we are no longer defined by our sin. This means that sin doesn't apply only to the creation of books, movies, and music that are fifty shades of creepy. It applies to "Christian" art, too. Some genuinely excellent creative efforts overtly point toward God as though their creators were saying, "Look how amazing God is!" Other works function as an opportunity for their creators to shout from the rooftops, "Look at how great I am!" The majority of human creative works exist somewhere in between. They have points at which they (intentionally or otherwise) reflect something of God's nature and character, even as they also have elements that obscure the truth of God.

We have to consider the message and what's behind everything we read, watch, listen to, or create, and how it shapes us. A few questions that help us in this include:

- What is it trying to communicate?

- What is its ultimate truth, and how does that truth reflect or conflict with what we know about God, ourselves, and the world he made?

- In what ways does this help me to love God more, and in what ways does it distract me from him?

It might seem restrictive to ask questions like this of everything, but it's actually the opposite. Thinking critically is liberating. Asking good questions of pop culture results in a creative world that is far more open than anyone could imagine.

Different needs in different seasons. Quality and content are key, but there are different times for every kind of pop culture and creative endeavor. As a new Christian, there might be music that you don't believe you can listen to in good conscience. Ditto books and movies. If you feel that way, follow it—that's an example of something called conviction, which is where the Holy Spirit prompts you to recognize something is right or wrong for you in that moment. But you may also find that your conviction will change over time, and music and movies you felt uncomfortable listening to in the past are open to you now (and the reverse is also true—sometimes what seemed fine for us at one point in our lives becomes no longer so over time and with maturity).

When I became a Christian, I found there was some music I loved in my teens and early twenties that I couldn't listen to anymore. The content was too dark and despairing, too hopeless and joyless. I still can't listen to it to this day. But there's other music that I felt I had to stop listening to that I could resume enjoying after a break of several years. In both instances, no one told me I had to stop listening to this music. In the case of the nihilistic nonsense I listened to in my youth, hopelessness no longer reflects who I am on any level. In the case of the other music I listened to and eventually came back to, I've been able to find a new appreciation for it. While the vast majority of what I listen to does not reflect my faith (the same is true of my engagement with books, movies, and TV), the act of engaging with good creative works—regardless of the background of their makers—has increased my love for God. Creativity is a gift from God to all who bear his image. Just as God can glorify himself through a sunset, so too can he glorify himself through a comic book, sci-fi movie, or rock-and-roll record. You can glorify him in enjoying those, too.

MODERN LOVE

//

CONFESSIONS, CONCESSIONS, AND UNTANGLING THE TANGLY BITS OF COHABITATION

I asked Emily to marry me (the first time) at the end of 2002. For several months, we'd been talking about the idea of marriage in general terms. What was her ideal kind of proposal; if we were to get married, would it be a big fancy wedding or something small and officiated at city hall? But it was all noncommittal conversation. Here's what she made clear:

1. Nothing in public.

2. Nothing fancy.

3. Nothing overly romantic.

I believed this was true. Because I'm an idiot.

So I asked her on a Friday night in December, maybe a couple of weeks before Christmas. We came home from a date, and as we got ready for bed, I brought out the ring and asked the big question. She fluttered her hands. Tears filled her eyes. She nodded and said yes. Then we went to sleep.

Nicholas Sparks has nothing on me.

Years later, Emily wished there was more of an exciting and memorable story to share with our children.[1] Knowing what I know now, there are a number of other things I would have done differently if I could go back in time. Yes, the proposal would be different. (In fact, we *did* have a super low-key reproposal in 2005 after we came to faith, but it mostly revolved around who would kill us and/or never let us hear the end of it if we got married without telling anyone.) But I *might* have included a couple more traditional songs during the wedding ceremony,[2] and I almost certainly would have had our officiant go full evangelist in explaining how marriage and the gospel connect (more on that in a minute). But of all the things I think Emily and I would have done differently, at the top of the list is how we dealt with the issue of our living arrangements.

HOW COHABITATION WON THE WEST

Emily and I lived together for several years before we were married. But it's not just that we lived together: we owned a house together. We worked for the same company and drove to work together every day in the car that we leased together. Our entire lives were intertwined because, well, that's what happens when you live together. The idea of living together before marrying wasn't foreign in our families. Cohabitation was normal. My parents lived together before marrying and divorced before I

---

1. It wouldn't have been as elaborate as what my friend Joe did when he proposed to his wife—he made a memory book with illustrations, poetry, photos, and even sewn elements! He successfully made every other man in the world look like a chump. But it's cool, Joe. It's cool. (Narrator: "But it wasn't cool.")
2. Though I stand by using "No Sissies" by Hawksley Workman for our recessional. Give it a listen, and I'm sure you'll see why I'm right: https://www.youtube.com/watch?v=gHoGH1oFURw.

started grade school, meaning the nuclear family was something I saw on television rather than experienced. Emily's parents lived together for several years before they got married as well (they remain married to this day). Siblings, extended family members, friends, coworkers—by the time I was twenty-five, I'm pretty sure I knew more people who were cohabitating with a significant other than were married. After we'd been dating for a while and wanted to take the next step in our relationship, that next step wasn't marriage. It was living together. Because that's what you do, right?

I doubt any of this is a surprise to you (except, possibly, my being so open about it). In fact, I'm willing to bet that you have cohabitated with someone you're not married to—or are doing so right now. If so, you're doing the same thing as many unmarried people in the United States, Canada, England, and most of the Western world. In the United States alone, people continue to marry later in life, and cohabitation is rapidly becoming the most common living arrangement (apart from living with parents).[3] But that doesn't mean such people are avoiding romantic relationships. They're just not getting married.

But have you ever asked why? Why is cohabitation the norm? Why is it seen as either the next step to marriage—or an alternative to it? Even among professing Christians, especially younger Christians, less mature Christians, and less engaged Christians, there is an increasing tendency to see nothing wrong with cohabitation at all, despite its negative effects on divorce rates and

---

3. The 2018 Census data indicates that only 29 percent of young adults (18–34) are married, a 30 percent decrease since 1978. Nine percent of young adults ages 18–24 live with an unmarried partner, versus 7 percent living with a spouse in 2018. For more information, see United States Census Bureau, "US Census Bureau Releases 2018 Family and Living Arrangements Tables," November 14, 2018, https://www.census.gov/newsroom/press-releases/2018/families.html.

overall societal health and cohesion.[4] It ultimately comes down to the replacement and devaluing of sex's intended context, which is revealed on two fronts.

CONSENT IS THE CONTEXT

The first is that sex doesn't have a context. Now, I had what most people would consider an atypical childhood, even by the standards of those who grew up in the 1980s. I was exposed to overtly sexual content at a very young age (like, four or five). Pornography was something I was at least passingly familiar with by my twelfth birthday.[5] I was pretty confused about sex and sexuality as a result. Being a natural researcher, I started trying to learn whether sex had any sort of context—whats, whens, with whoms—all that kind of stuff. Turns out, I wasn't the only one confused.

Once upon a time, there was a generally agreed-on understanding within Western society about the context of sex. This understanding was rooted in the Bible's teaching and said that sex was to be enjoyed solely within the bounds of marriage. While there has never been a time when sex was consistently limited to this context, the idea was at least present in our collective minds for generations. However, from the 1960s through the 1990s, that understanding of the proper context for sex was reduced from marriage to being ready to have sex. I remember learning in my sex-education classes about how our bodies

---

4. According to one study, 45 percent of cohabiting couples who marry eventually divorce. Meanwhile, 79 percent of marriages among those who did not cohabitate prior to marriage remain intact. For more, see David J. Ayers, "The Cohabitation Dilemma Comes for America's Pastors," *Christianity Today*, March 16, 2021, https://www.christianitytoday.com/ct/2021/april/cohabitation-dilemma-comes-for-american-pastors-ayers.html.
5. While this is hardly uncommon today, remember: I was born in 1979. Such things were not nearly as readily available.

change in puberty, and there was some clinical discussion about mechanics led by a visibly uncomfortable gym teacher, and a few of the consequences were addressed as well. However, the only context we were offered was this vague idea of being ready. (I once asked a teacher how you knew whether you were ready. The teacher responded, "When you don't have to ask that question." That did not really clear anything up for me.)

But ready is at least a better answer than what's offered today. It implies a certain level of maturity and maybe even a relationship. Now sex is so removed from any meaningful context that relationships, intimacy, and even names are no longer essential. Finding a willing partner just requires swiping right. Essentially, the context for sex can be summed up in one word: consent. No emotional involvement required. It's just physical. Because it's just physical, as long as those involved agree, you're good to go.

Interestingly, the concept of consent today owes its very existence to Christianity.[6] Within Roman culture, consent wasn't really a thing; lower classes were subject to the whims of the upper classes, who, legally if not morally, had the freedom to have sex with whomever and whatever they pleased. Christians, on the other hand, held (and hold) a radical perspective on sex and intimacy, in that both parties ought to be willing participants

6. "True consent was a rarity in the world in which Christianity got its start. Christianity, we might say, invented consensual sex when it developed a sex ethic that assumed God empowers individuals with freedom." Beth Felker Jones, *Mark of His Wounds: Gender Politics and Bodily Resurrection* (Oxford: Oxford University Press, 2007), 80, as quoted in Nancy Pearcey, *Love Thy Body: Answering Hard Truths about Life and Sexuality* (Grand Rapids: Baker, 2018), 143.

(that both husbands and wives are engaged and willing, as in 1 Corinthians 7:3–4).[7]

THE MEANING(LESSNESS) OF MARRIAGE

If sex being without a context is one problem, the meaning of marriage is the other—or rather, the meaninglessness. Western people once shared a definition of marriage that was rooted in the Bible's understanding (the lifelong union between one man and one woman for the propagation and flourishing of humanity).[8] But over time that shared understanding has been replaced with a more fluid perspective, to the point that there is no generally agreed-on consensus, beyond the union of people creating rights and obligations between them.

Basically, marriage is a contract to be renewed, broken, and completed as one or more of those bound by it choose. The contract can be ended for any reason, whether valid and biblically defensible (such as abuse, adultery, and abandonment) to the ill-defined (the oft-heard irreconcilable differences) and outright ridiculous (such as one spouse asking what the other wants in his coffee every morning for seven years).[9] Put simply, we

7. On this point, it's worth stating that there are some who have interpreted 1 Corinthians 7's teaching as a refutation of the concept of mutual consent within marriage. But 1 Corinthians 7 only refutes the necessity of marital consent if you ignore the second half of verse 3 and the second half of verse 4—husbands and wives belong to one another, not as property, but as partners. So if you ever run across teaching like that, run for the hills. It is straight from the pit of hell.
8. This is why Christians typically use the word covenant instead of contract to describe the nature of marriage. A covenant is best understood to be an ongoing promise, whereas a contract is a limited agreement.
9. I'm not even kidding. See Asia McLain, "17 Divorce Lawyers Shared the Weirdest Reasons People Got Divorced and I Don't Know What to Say," Buzzfeed, January 28, 2020, https://www.buzzfeed.com/asiawmclain/divorce-reasons. Keep this article in mind if you encounter someone who says the husband's desires in this area take precedence. Also, guys, don't be that guy. And ladies, don't be involved with that guy.

have greater legal obligations to our landlords than we do to our spouses. (And all who have ever broken a lease said, "Amen.")

Put these two issues together—sex without context and marriage with no meaning—and you have the hot mess that you may well find yourself in today.

WHAT NEEDED TO BE SPELLED OUT FOR ME (AND PROBABLY FOR YOU)

Depending on how far you've gotten into your Bible at this point, you may or may not be surprised to learn that it has a lot to say about what happens in the bedroom. The Bible describes sexual intimacy as a good gift, something to be enjoyed (Song of Solomon 1:2, 13; 2:3, 6; 4:5). It is something to be enjoyed within a very specific context: marriage between one man and one woman (Genesis 2:24; Matthew 19:5–6; 1 Corinthians 6:16).[10] It is an expression of love and desire for your spouse (1 Corinthians 7:9). It is the means by which we have children and fulfill the command to "be fruitful and multiply" (Genesis 1:28). It is something to be enjoyed joyfully, freely, and as frequently as *both* husband and wife desire (1 Corinthians 7:3–6).

Okay, I know I've just written a bunch about sex in that paragraph, but even with all that, you also need to know that sex is *not* the point of marriage. Marriage is not about sex; marriage is

---

10. Although it goes well beyond the scope of this book, you should know the Bible also expressly prohibits same-sex relationships in multiple Old and New Testament passages: Genesis 19; Leviticus 18:22; 20:13; Romans 1:18–32 (particularly verses 26–27); 1 Corinthians 6:9–10; and 1 Timothy 1:10. Though there are some professing Christians who challenge the meaning of these verses, they do so only by engaging in extraordinary feats of exegetical gymnastics. The clarity and consistency with which the Bible speaks on this matter is honestly incredible. For two excellent nontechnical treatments of this subject, I recommend Kevin DeYoung, *What Does the Bible Really Teach about Homosexuality* (Wheaton, IL: Crossway, 2015), and Sam Allberry, *Is God Anti-Gay?* (Epsom, UK: Good Book, 2014).

the context for it. The point of marriage, its meaning, has to do with the gospel itself. Marriage is a living illustration of the gospel for the world to see.[11] Paul wrote that Jesus "loved the church and gave himself for her to make her holy" (Ephesians 5:25–26). He came into the world out of love for his bride, and rescued her by dying on the cross and rising again from the dead. Jesus helps her to become "without spot or blemish" (2 Peter 3:14), set apart and pure, so that on the day he comes back into the world, they will be joined in what the Bible calls the "marriage feast of the Lamb" (Revelation 19:9), and everyone who has ever believed in Jesus ever will be there to celebrate it.

This is why the Bible describes sex and marriage as something to be honored, protected, and kept pure (Hebrews 13:1–5). It is also why the Bible includes several prohibitions related to sex. God doesn't call us to be prudes; he expects us to honor his intentions for the good things he has made. This is why Paul, one of the church's earliest leaders, told Christians in many different cities to abstain from sexual immorality (1 Thessalonians 4:3)—in fact, he told us to *flee*, or run away, from it (1 Corinthians 6:18). But what is sexual immorality? The phrase is kind of a junk-drawer term for all kinds of sexual behavior that is outside God's intentions: sex outside marriage (both premarital sex and adultery), pornography, same-sex relationships, and everything that happens on *The Bachelor*.[12] Basically everything that you and I would have given exactly zero thought to before Jesus saved us and everything the culture we live in celebrates on a daily basis.

---

11. An outstanding book on this subject is Timothy Keller and Kathy Keller, *The Meaning of Marriage* (New York: Penguin Random House, 2015).
12. Throughout Paul's letters to different churches, he describes Christians having been engaged in all of these behaviors in the past. "And some of you used to be like this," he writes in 1 Corinthians 6:11. Take that to heart: no one is so sinful that God's grace can't take hold of them.

THE HEART OF THE MATTER

I've met a lot of Christians who either grew up going to church or have been following Jesus for a long time who struggle to understand why the Bible's way of talking about sex isn't obvious to everyone. But what they often forget is that the very idea that God actually cares at all about sex is foreign to most of us. So, when we read the Bible for the first time, its prohibitions against polygamy, homosexuality, and adultery—along with bestiality and incest—can be mistaken for relics from an ancient culture (Exodus 20:14; Leviticus 18:6–23). After all, we don't wear head coverings (1 Corinthians 11:2–14), some of us eat shellfish and bacon (Leviticus 11:1–47), and the majority of us probably wear mixed fabrics from time to time (Leviticus 19:19; Deuteronomy 22:11).[13] But what is easily missed by many readers—whether established Christians, new believers, or non-Christians—in these apparent cultural relics is their larger context, the same one that ultimately governs sex and marriage as well: worship.[14]

The Old Testament connects sex to worship in explicit commands and in commentary on the acts of the Israelites

13. Food laws in the Old Testament were intended to show Israel's separation from the nations. The matter of head coverings is a cultural example that points to a universal reality, that Christians are to embrace the God-given distinctions between men and women rather than downplaying or denying them, as was happening in Corinth in Paul's day (and continues into our own). The prohibition regarding mixed fabrics is specific to wool and linen; its intent is debated, but the general consensus suggests a connection to maintaining God's standards of holiness (avoiding idolatry and maintaining distinction from the world). See Eugene H. Merrill, *Deuteronomy*, New American Commentary 4 (Nashville: B&H Academic, 1994).

14. Based on the way movements such as True Love Waits speak about sex (a part of 1980s and 1990s purity culture—the stuff us adult converts missed by either not being born or being godless heathens), I get the impression that most established Christians don't understand this either. Too often we can speak about sex in terms of worship, but we do this by elevating sex outside its context of worshiping God and as something that is meant to be worshiped (or demonized).

(Exodus 34:15; Deuteronomy 23:17; Judges 2:17; 2 Chronicles 21:11).[15] The New Testament doubles down on this, especially in the book of Romans, where sexual immorality in general, and same-sex relationships, in particular, are described as one of the primary fruits of refusing to acknowledge and honor God (Romans 1:18–31).[16] While these are negative examples, don't forget: the Bible speaks positively about sex too (all those points I mentioned a few pages ago). It's just a question of in what context. But the positive or negative examples point us to the same truth—sex is an act of worship.

CONFRONTING THE ELEPHANT IN OUR BEDROOM

Now, after reading all that, there's a good chance you're feeling a bit uncomfortable. You've likely never thought about sex from this perspective, and you almost certainly haven't lived up to this standard (but it's okay: most people who grew up going to church haven't either). But I'm not sharing any of this to make you feel guilt or shame. When it comes to just about every area of the Christian life where we are out of step with God's intention, there will be moments where we feel something called *conviction*. This means that we realize that we have done (or are doing) something wrong, and something needs to change. That takes time.

---

15. In these passages, the Israelites are forbidden from being cult prostitutes (who used sex as part of a fertility rite in Canaanite worship), and Israel's worship of false gods is likened to prostitution.
16. The question of same-sex relationships is one that you will be confronted with over the course of your life as a Christian, and it needs to be handled sensitively and respectfully. Sam Allberry, a British pastor who experiences same-sex attraction, has written two excellent short books on the subject that do exactly that: *Is God Anti-Gay?* (Epsom, UK: Good Book, 2014), and *Why Does God Care Who I Sleep With?* (Epsom, UK: Good Book, 2020).

For me, conviction about this issue came both gradually *and* suddenly. There were certain things that no one had to tell either me or Emily were wrong. No one had to tell us that pornography was a bad thing and something that shouldn't be in our lives. We came to that conclusion on our own pretty quickly. But when it came to our living arrangements in general, and sharing a bedroom in particular, well that took a bit more time.

For our first few weeks as Christians, we more or less continued to live the way we had before. We weren't intentionally defying God by doing so; we just didn't know better. It was sin committed in ignorance. We had not yet grasped that Jesus was the Lord of our bedroom.

So, the Lord sent an elephant juggling a ton of bricks while standing on a piano to delicately graze our respective craniums.

It was a sunny August day when Emily and I got a call from Emily's mother. At work. She called to let us know that Emily's sister had become sexually active with her boyfriend.[17] After we were kind of grossed out for a bit—because who likes to think of their siblings doing things that are only okay for *them* to do— we realized something: if we weren't okay with her doing that, why was it okay for us?

And the elephant whooshed passed us.

We emailed our pastor and told him we needed to meet after work. We drove over, the ick factor still high, wondering how we were going to tell him what happened and whether he would have any idea what we should do. We came into his office, more or less complete messes, and told him everything that happened—the call, realizing that we were in a jam and didn't know what to do.

---

17. And yes, my mother-in-law really did describe it that way. Imagine Grandpa Simpson saying this, and you'll have a sense of the discomfort we felt.

Do you know what he did?

He laughed. Seriously!

He didn't do it in a malicious way. He was delighted because we weren't the only couple in the church dealing with this. There were a whole bunch of brand-new Christians there, who were all in relationships where we lived together, slept together, and then, suddenly, believed together. As delighted as he was that a bunch of twenty-somethings all suddenly believed in Jesus, he also knew that our living arrangements were a recipe for disaster. So, he found himself with a choice to make: How was he going to address the fact that a bunch of recovering sinners were still sinning? The way I see it, he had a few different options. He could have met with all of us and said, "Hey dummies, quit doing that right now." He wouldn't have been wrong to do that. But he didn't. He could have also started a sermon series called something like: "Seven Steps to a Godly Sex Life," with step 1 being, "If you're not married but living with someone, get married!" He probably wouldn't have been wrong to do that either. But instead, he did something much better and more effective. Something so revolutionary and yet so obvious that most of us forget that it's even an option:

He prayed.

He asked God to intervene and for the Holy Spirit to convict the lot of us. And wouldn't you know it? God answered.

By convicting me and Emily.

The ones with a mortgage who worked at the same company and drove to work together every day in the car they leased together. The ones with tons of consumer debt and student debt on top of that. The ones who were about as entangled as people can get without having children.

The ones sitting in our pastor's office, confused as all get-out as he laughed over how God answered his prayer. After he told us all of this, I asked, "So what should we do?"

"What do *you* think you should do?" he replied.

"We don't know—that's why we're asking you!"

We walked through all the details of our situation together. We talked about finances, the house, the works. Eventually one of us (I don't remember who) said, "I know this isn't ideal, but there are multiple bedrooms in the house. Could we make it work if we kept to separate rooms?"

CONCESSIONS AND GRACE

"You're right, it's not ideal," he said. He was right, for all the reasons I shared before about the context of sex and the meaning of marriage. He could have countered with another option. He could have told us to consider getting married that weekend. He also could have said that one of us should find another place to live until we were ready to get married.

But he didn't do either.

Instead, he said, "But we can work with that."

Why would our pastor say that—why would he go along with something that he knew had a chance of going really, really badly? I never asked him (which I should have done), but if I had to guess, here's my hunch: he was showing grace to a couple of brand-new baby Christians. He had already seen God answering his prayers for us. Conviction had come, just as he asked. We realized our living situation was not right, and we were trying to figure out how to honor God in the middle of a mess. But that grace included some strict ground rules:

1. Under no circumstances were we to be in each other's rooms.

2. There would be no allowance for any kind of romantic situations. If one presented itself, I was to leave and not return until things cooled down.

3. We needed friends from the church who would have their homes open to me if we were at risk of violating rule 2.

4. We had to have an open-book policy with our pastor and our friends: any of them could ask us about anything at any time.

5. We had to join a small group for newly married couples and couples pursuing marriage.

6. We had to participate in premarital counseling, with another couple discipling us through the process.

It wouldn't have been gracious of our pastor to let us go on our merry way. That would have been devastating to us and left us in a position where we would have violated God's commands related to sex. Instead, we had a situation that was not ideal, but one that we honored, as my friends who hosted me when I'd show up with Starbucks in hand at 10 p.m. can attest.

But just because it worked doesn't make it right.

Our living arrangement in that season as unmarried brand-new Christians was a concession. The closest example I can find in the Bible comes from the examples of polygamy among the patriarchs and Israel's kings, even as the Bible itself explicitly condemns such acts (Deuteronomy 17:17). Some of the great heroes of the faith, including Abraham, Jacob, David, and Solomon, were hardly one-woman men. Abraham took Hagar as his concubine at the request of Sarah (Genesis 16) and had multiple wives after Sarah's death. Jacob took both Rachel and Leah as his wives, and then their servants, Bilhah and Zilpah, were brought into the mix as well (Genesis 29–30). David had many wives and concubines, though we're never told exactly how many (2 Samuel 5:13).[18] His son Solomon took the ball and ran with it, taking for himself more than seven hundred wives and three hundred concubines (1 Kings 11:3). But never once, anywhere in all of Scripture, do we read that these things pleased the Lord. They happened, but that doesn't make them right. At the same time, we should also remember how much grace God showed each of them. God didn't abandon Abraham, Jacob, David, Solomon, or any of the others who compromised themselves through their sinful choices. He used them to fulfill his plans to save sinners like you and me through the life, death, and resurrection of Jesus—in fact, all of them are a part of Jesus's family line!

You and I are not those people, but the principle applies: God brought Jesus into the world through messed-up people. God saves messed-up people through Jesus. And God makes Jesus known to messed-up people using the messed-up people he saves. If God showed grace to polygamists, murderers, and well, Solomon, he has ample grace for you and me too. That grace involves making some decisions to get out of a compromised situation.

UNTANGLING THE TANGLY BITS (OR HOW TO ESCAPE THE COHABITATION TRAP)

If you're living with someone you're not married to, if you're sleeping with someone who isn't your spouse, something needs to change. But what's the best way forward?

First, while every situation is unique and needs to be addressed in partnership with your church leaders, every

---

18. Of his many wives, eight are mentioned by name: Michal (1 Samuel 18–19; 2 Samuel 3), Abigail (1 Samuel 25), Bathsheba (2 Samuel 11:1–17), Ahinoam, Maacah, Haggith, Abital, and Eglah (2 Samuel 3:2–5; 1 Chronicles 3:1–3).

solution starts with prayer. You need to pray that the Holy Spirit will give you and others the wisdom and support necessary to help you to live a holy, uncompromised life in this area. You may not have had a lot of experience with this yet, but trust me: he will give you everything you need.

Second, as I've considered my own situation, seen others walk through similar ones, and spoken with pastors over the years, I've consistently seen three options emerge as the most common ways to respond faithfully to conviction about cohabitation.

1. Get married as soon as possible. This is often the go-to response from Christians who have not lived in a culture where cohabitation is normal. There are some couples who choose to do this, and for many of them it's the right thing to do—especially if they already have or are expecting children. Of all the options, this probably has the least chance of complications for you, though it may have the most significant relational consequences (such as people being upset they weren't invited to the wedding because it was super small).

Believe it or not, around the same time we were convicted of our cohabitating lifestyle, Emily and I did have a discussion about what might happen if we "got married tomorrow." Even though we were open to the idea, we also felt it was not right, and our pastor agreed. We needed the time leading up to our wedding to get to know one another again as the new creations we were (and are). We needed to talk through and pray about issues that had never really been conversations to that point (such as children). Then there would have been the family drama that we'd have had to deal with. And maybe it's selfish, but we didn't want to have to hear about how we didn't invite anyone to our wedding during every major family get-together for the rest of our lives (and positively, the discussion we had about getting married quickly did result in our low-key reproposal and setting a date).

How do you know whether this is the right solution for you? In order to answer that question, you need outside wisdom. You need to pray, and you need to talk to your pastor together with your significant other. If both of you love Jesus and you agree on many of the core fundamentals that are often conflict points in marriage—especially views on divorce and whether to have children—then mainly you're good to go. But if you don't have those fundamentals worked out ahead of time, it's probably better to wait and go a different route.

2. End the relationship. While getting married is the right call for many couples caught in cohabitation as new believers, it's not for all. In fact, it is foolish to assume that just because two people are romantically involved before coming to faith that their relationship should continue. When a foundational shift such as becoming a Christian happens, we have to reexamine everything, including our relationships. While some relationships grow and become stronger as a result, others need to be dissolved—especially if your relationship has been characterized by discord, infidelity, abuse,[19] or your significant other is not a Christian.[20]

In choosing this option, you're going to have a lot of work to do, including:

- Selling a home (if you own one together) or breaking/renegotiating your lease.

---

19. I believe that while God can redeem and restore relationships where terrible things have happened, separation is an absolute must as a starting point. If you are in an abusive relationship, get out now.
20. While I haven't addressed this issue in our discussion, you should know that being romantically involved with or married to a non-Christian generally does not work out well. Ending this sort of relationship should be handled in as loving and respectful a situation as possible.

- Detangling your lives, separating finances, redistributing possessions.

- Explaining why you're ending the relationship to a lot of people who may be disappointed.

That third point above isn't all bad: as you explain to people why your relationship is ending, you'll have the opportunity to share Jesus with them. (Okay, maybe that's not super comforting, but it's still true.)

It wasn't until I wrote the first version of this chapter several years ago that I learned from Emily this question was running through her mind during the time leading up to our marriage: Should she marry me? Was I really the man that she should spend the rest of her life with? What if our faith was leading us in different directions? Thankfully, the Lord deemed it favorable that she should remain with this knucklehead. I think (I hope) she'd tell you she's happy with the life she has being married to me.

How do you know whether this is the solution for you? Well, it depends. If your relationship has already been unhealthy and destructive, then it's probably pretty cut-and-dried. You should split up. But, like Emily and me, the answer one way or the other can only come with time, prayer, and counsel.

3. *Live apart while rebuilding the relationship.* Of all the options I've shared, this one is probably the best of them. But it is also the most challenging, and not just because of the financial implications (although there are a whole lot of those). In this situation, you may need to consider selling a home altogether or finding a sublessee for your apartment or a short-term roommate while one of you moves out. It means figuring out a new place for one of you to live, whether renting a room with a family from church, moving back in with parents, or even staying with a friend should one be kind enough to help in this way. It means reworking your budget in order to carry on with preexisting financial commitments (for example, a mortgage or car payment). In the same way you would if you had broken up, you will have to deal with people looking at you like you've got two heads. After all, this is the most countercultural—and least convenient—option. But it may be the one that most overtly says, "Yes, Jesus is Lord, including over my bedroom."

Now, you probably noticed that I didn't mention that we rejected the idea of living apart earlier. That's because it was never brought up. It didn't occur to me or Emily, and the idea wasn't raised by our pastor. Why? I'm not sure. As I said before, my hunch is that he was showing grace to a couple of messed up brand-new baby Christians. What do I think I would have said if he had asked? In all honesty, I don't know. I hope I would have said yes and then asked how we could make it happen. But the truth is I will never know. (That's the tough thing about the past, isn't it? You can't go back and change it, so there's no point in playing "what if" games.)

So, how do you know whether this is the solution for you? Let me put it this way, understanding that I sound like a hypocrite: if you and your significant other need time while planning for marriage and relearning one another in light of being Christians, then this is the option for you. But here's the thing: for this to work, your church needs to help you. If you are at a church where the people know you and are invested in you (like the type of church I recommended you look for in chapter 3), then they need to do more than just tell you to live apart or get married. They need to work with you to figure out how to make the situation work in a way where God will get the most glory. (For the leaders reading this, I have a few ideas that I'll share at the end of the book.)

GRACE ABOUNDS IN THE MESS

Up to now, I've only told you the options that I see available based on my experience. Maybe you wish I would tell you specifically what to do. But there's a reason I'm not going to: I don't know your situation. You might be living with someone, and the best thing for you is to put down this book, get in the car, and go get married. But that might be exactly the wrong thing, too.

I can only tell you to pray, talk to your friends, and talk to your pastor(s). They will hopefully know your situation far better than someone you've never met. Pray with them. Listen to them. But also recognize that there are no easy answers to these kinds of situations. If you're committed to following Jesus, just know that there will be much grace for you in the mess. Jesus is Lord of all, including your bedroom. I have no doubt that you will see him work powerfully in your life even through difficult decisions that will bring you closer to him.

7

SAVE IT FOR LATER

//

IT'S TOO SOON FOR YOU TO LEAD

I've made a lot of mistakes in my life—and in my life as a Christian. Not leaving a church at the right time, making poor choices around my marriage proposal, and trying to like terrible Christian music are just a few of the blunders I've made. But one of the worst was not realizing I was too immature to be a leader in the church.

As a brand-new Christian, while in the middle of the giant mess of trying to figure out what that even meant, our church's kids' ministry leader asked me to serve there. But it wasn't just to serve as a helper. It was to help *lead* the fourth- and fifth-grade class. Talk about the Bible passage, facilitate the discussion, pray with the kids, stuff like that. Within a year of coming to faith, after attending the men's ministry breakfasts on a regular basis, one of the leaders asked me to join its leadership team. A year after that, he handed over the reins of the entire ministry to me. Around the same time, I started leading a Bible study group, filled almost exclusively with other twenty-somethings who were either new believers or professing believers who were even less mature in their faith than I was.

To that point, I had shown a great deal of excitement about my faith, and I was reading my Bible fairly regularly, even if I was still asking, "What does this mean for me right now?" People further along in the faith were excited about me—and not just because of the novelty of a person coming to faith as an adult. They started to see hints of what God might be doing, some of them recognizing gifts he was giving me that I didn't even recognize, and they were trying to steer me onto the right path.

Unfortunately, the thing no one was considering was my character. Which is a shame, because I was becoming a bit of a jerk. I started to think I was a big deal while also believing I was the absolute worst as I muddled through every moment. But because no one, not even my pastor, was saying, "Hey, maybe slow down," I didn't know there was a problem. Not at first, anyway.

THE LOW BAR FOR CHRISTIAN LEADERSHIP

So why was no one saying no? Why were people letting and encouraging a guy who eighteen months earlier had not even *opened* a Bible lead Bible studies? Why would anyone let a joker who didn't know the first thing about being a faithful Christian man be responsible for a ministry that was supposed to be built around that? It all seems unwise.

And it was.

But it also wasn't uncommon. It still isn't because many churches have a low bar for deciding who can or should serve in or lead a ministry. Here are the three most commonly used criteria:

They're excited. Excitement is a good thing. Hopefully at this stage, as a relatively new Christian, you're excited about your faith. You should be! But being pumped about Jesus isn't enough to put someone in a leadership role in the church. Eventually, excitement fades, and what remains when it does?

SAVE IT FOR LATER

They're willing. Sometimes leaders are chosen because they say yes. That's how I ended up leading a small group. It's how I was teaching in the kids' ministry. It's why I was on the leadership team for the men's ministry when I was a year into my faith. In every instance, it was because someone asked, and I said yes. But is that enough?

They're alive. Also known as the "mirror test" (because if you're breathing you'll fog up a mirror), this is the most common way many churches find leaders and volunteers for certain ministries, especially kids' ministry. If volunteers are breathing and profess to be Christians, they're in.

But these three criteria—excitement, willingness, and being alive—aren't the best criteria for identifying leaders in our churches. It's not good for the church, and it's not good for anyone put in that position. (It certainly wasn't good for me.) These criteria place the bar far too low in an area where the Bible places the bar exceptionally and necessarily high.

THE HIGH BAR OF CHRISTIAN LEADERSHIP

There's a tendency among Christians who write on leadership to take the best practices of the business marketplace and Christianize them. We will say, for example, that casting a compelling vision is important and attach a verse such as Proverbs 29:18 to it ("Where there is no vision, the people perish" [KJV]), even if it's not what the verse means.[1] But this isn't the way the Bible should be used, as a validation for a belief we already hold to. Instead, we have to read the Bible on its own terms—to take

---

1. This verse, which reads in full, "Without revelation people run wild, but one who follows divine instruction will be happy" (CSB), is referring to the centrality of God's word to the life of his people. It's also worth noting that we should avoid using proverbs for prooftexts when making definitive statements, since, by definition, a proverb is proverbial—it is a truism, not a promise.

what it says, try to understand what it meant to its original audience as best as we are able, and then apply the relevant principles to our context. When we do that, we see that the Bible says a lot about the qualities of good leaders. What it says can be summed up in one word: character.

Think about the book of Proverbs, which is a book compiling wise sayings from primarily King Solomon, along with a few others. In its pages, there are many proverbs offered about the importance of character. For example:

People of character are people of integrity:

> A good name is to be chosen over great wealth; favor is better than silver and gold. (Proverbs 22:1)

> The one who lives with integrity lives securely, but whoever perverts his ways will be found out. (Proverbs 10:9)

Developing character requires community:

> A fool's way is right in his own eyes, but whoever listens to counsel is wise. (Proverbs 12:15)

> Arrogance leads to nothing but strife, but wisdom is gained by those who take advice. (Proverbs 13:10)

Developing character requires humility:

> When arrogance comes, disgrace follows, but with humility comes wisdom. (Proverbs 11:2)

> Pride comes before destruction, and an arrogant spirit before a fall. (Proverbs 16:18)

There are other examples of individuals who demonstrated the kind of character that Christian leaders should pursue and possess. But there's one passage in the New Testament that makes this point unmistakably clear—and it's among the most-cited passages on this subject.

First Timothy 3:2–7 is the go-to passage to describe the qualities of a Christian leader (and specifically of a pastor). In a passage like this, you might expect that Paul would be concerned with skills—administrative abilities, teaching quality, being a visionary leader, and stuff like that. Instead, he wrote something entirely unlike what you or I probably would:

> An overseer, therefore, must be above reproach, the husband of one wife, self-controlled, sensible, respectable, hospitable, able to teach, not an excessive drinker, not a bully but gentle, not quarrelsome, not greedy. He must manage his own household competently and have his children under control with all dignity. (If anyone does not know how to manage his own household, how will he take care of God's church?) He must not be a new convert, or he might become conceited and incur the same condemnation as the devil. Furthermore, he must have a good reputation among outsiders, so that he does not fall into disgrace and the devil's trap. (1 Timothy 3:2–7)

This passage contains somewhere in the neighborhood of fourteen characteristics of a faithful leader. Of those fourteen, only one is an actual skill—the ability to teach. Everything else focuses on character. In fact, the first line, which says that an overseer, or a pastor, must be above reproach, is the master definition. Being a person of good character, of integrity, is essential to being a Christian leader, and everything else Paul wrote in this list is a specific example of how that integrity is demonstrated in a person's life.

So Christian leaders are faithful to their spouses, reflecting the relationship between Jesus and the church (Ephesians 5:25).[2] Christian leaders are to be self-controlled and not prone to overindulgence or fits of rage. They're to have good common sense, be people worthy of respect, and be welcoming of others. They're not to be people who court controversy and go looking for fights (or creating them). They aren't culture warriors, but they are peacemakers (Matthew 5:9; Romans 12:18). They're not in ministry to make a name for themselves and use the church as a way to get rich. In other words, a true church leader is a person of character. This is the most important thing leaders can be.

Yet, it's the thing that more established Christians pay less attention to than anything else. Sure, there's lip service given to its importance, but ask someone in your church what makes a good leader. You're undoubtedly going to hear them talk about a leader's ability to teach. What is the pastor's preaching like? How interesting/informative/entertaining is it? Sometimes they'll branch out and talk about their ability to lead through a crisis, cast vision, and so forth, but at the end of the day, teaching ability is looked at as what matters. This belief is what contributes to the problem of the low bar for leadership because it puts the emphasis on the wrong syllable, as it were. Teaching abilities matter, absolutely. But a person might be able to teach, be a great visionary, or highly administrative, but might also be a narcissist, arrogant, spiritually abusive, manipulative, a lover of money, prone to outbursts of anger, or quarrelsome. If they're any of these things, how well they teach doesn't matter at all. People of questionable character, people who lack integrity, have no business leading any part of a church in any capacity.

2. This also applies to unmarried leaders, in that they're not to be engaged with any kind of immoral sexual behavior of any kind (like the rest of us).

THE STANDARD OF SPIRITUAL MATURITY

Now, you're probably not being asked to be a pastor at this stage in your life. (At least I hope not.) But even though I've said a lot that might look like it applies only to pastors, it applies to you too. It applies to all of us because the way the Bible describes the qualities of Christian leaders is no different from any of its descriptions of what any mature Christian should be. We are all called to be people of integrity, of strong character that has been (and continues to be) shaped by Jesus every day as we make him the focus of our lives.

That's why one other attribute that Paul mentions is super important: a church leader must not be a new convert. Not *should* not—*must* not. Why? This has nothing to do with age. It has everything to do with maturity as a Christian. Even though you as a new believer might be capable of leading, or even be a leader in your regular job, becoming a leader in church too soon puts you in danger of becoming prideful. Because here's the thing: the reason you might be asked to lead likely has nothing to do with your abilities and everything to do with your enthusiasm. You're passionate about your faith. You're excited about Jesus. You should be—the gospel is exciting! But it's not wise to take on responsibilities you're not ready for, whether you're twenty-five, forty-five, or sixty-five.

I needed to hear this when I was a new Christian because when I most needed to be sitting under someone's leadership—to be learning, growing, and building the foundation of my faith—I was trying to do that for others. And it was bad—so bad. The Lord graciously prevented me from doing serious damage to the faith of other believers (at least as far as I know), but wow, did I ever do a lot of damage to myself. I developed an extremely prideful attitude. I had a swagger that didn't befit a Christian. I had delusions of grandeur.

Now, here's the thing: I didn't start any of these things believing I was the cock of the walk. I started serving in children's ministry because I was asked. I started serving in the men's ministry leadership because I wanted to help people. I started a small group because there was a need. But if I'd had any common sense, I would never have done any of it at that point. I wish someone—specifically my pastor—had said to me, "You have learned much, young one, but you're not a leader yet." But that didn't happen. So, the Lord eventually had someone (or rather someones) say no to me. I just didn't expect the first to be my wife.

IMMATURITY CHALLENGED

One night after a particularly frustrating leadership team meeting, my wife said to me, "You need to quit." She then proceeded to outline all the concerns she had with how being in this role that I was unsuited for was affecting me. She saw how it was killing my joy, that it was a distraction from everything else I was good at, and that there was no real fruit coming from it. Of course, being self-righteous and stupid, I accused her of not supporting me and pouted about it—until I realized that her telling me to quit was her way of supporting me.

The second time came a few months later, as a friend and I were driving to a pastors' event in a neighboring city. We were talking about ministry and whether I'd ever be a good fit for being a pastor. He looked right at me and said, "Here's the thing: It's not that you're arrogant, but you certainly have the appearance of arrogance. And you need to work on that."

That hit me like a ton of bricks. I *was* arrogant (as he subtly told me without actually telling me). And I knew it wasn't okay. Something had to change. So, ever so slowly, it did, in part, because my friend told me what was wrong—and helped me work through it.

I first asked to be released from serving in the men's ministry. Then I ended my community group. I stepped away from serving in the children's ministry. I started focusing more on prayer and time in the Bible. I started spending time with older men who were willing to invest in me and help me grow as a Christian.

PURSUING CHARACTER AND MATURITY

Maybe you're already being encouraged to take on certain responsibilities. Maybe you've shown some potential in an area your church values, and you're wondering whether your potential means you should pursue some kind of leadership role. Let me tell you right now: no, you shouldn't. If you're only a short time into your life as a Christian, you don't want to get sucked into roles you're not ready for. But that doesn't mean never. It just means not right now. Between now and when you're ready, you need to focus on your character. Here are three ways to do that:

1. **Keep studying your Bible and growing in your prayer life.** These are the personal foundations of your life as a Christian, and they need to be prioritized. They're a key way that you grow in your knowledge of God and in your relationship with him.

2. **Serve in obscurity.** Don't worry about highly visible areas in the church. Look at the roles no one seems to want to do. If you've got a parking lot, maybe it's traffic management. If you've got a children's ministry, maybe it's as a classroom helper. Maybe it's on the setup team, or the cleaning crew, or the sound board. Whatever it is, serve somewhere quiet.

3. **Build relationships with more mature Christians in your church.** Learn from them. Open your life up to them. Let them speak into your life and character as you mature. Let them identify what they see as gifts God has given you to serve the church.

And in all this, be patient. If you have the potential to be a leader, perhaps God will give you the opportunity to lead. Whenever that is, *if* that ever is, remember: your character is what matters most. As you focus on developing as a person of integrity, as a person who is above reproach, you will be prepared to serve in every way God would have you.

8

PEOPLE ARE PEOPLE

//

HOW TO DISAGREE LIKE A CHRISTIAN

The Internet is a strange and wonderful place, giving you the ability simultaneously enjoy a much larger and much smaller world. If you want to talk to someone across the world, you can. If you want to learn literally anything, you can. If you want to find a community, you can (kind of).

For an introvert like me, the Internet, and particularly message boards, became a safe place in my teen years.[1] It was a digital haven in the storm of life. I wasn't comfortable talking to, well, anyone. But I could type. Because of that, I could be myself, as charismatic and amusing as it is possible to be clacking away on a keyboard. But it also wasn't long until I discovered what happens when you combine anonymity, an apparently consequence-free environment, and people with too much time on their hands. It could get ugly fast, as seemingly innocent comments erupted into

---

1. Message boards were the precursor to modern social media. There are a few of these online communities that still exist and are active, but they became passé around 2006, when Facebook became available to the world at large.

intense name-calling, character assassination, and occasionally real-life altercations. People said (and say) whatever they wanted, did whatever they wanted, were whomever they wanted, and thought they'd experience no repercussions in their real lives, Wheaton's Law be damned.[2]

Whether as a witness or an active participant, you've probably seen this type of behavior. It's tempting to think of it as a problem that exists purely within the online ecosystem. (If only things were that simple.) This problem goes beyond what we experience online and affects every interaction we have with other people because what happens online is a symptom of a larger sickness within Western culture as a whole: a collective, and perhaps unknowing, embrace of arrogant intolerance that requires absolute and unquestioning allegiance to one value or belief set, with no room for different perspectives. This mindset is deeply embedded into our culture—in our political discourse, in our entertainment, and, sadly, in our churches as well. It can leave us tense and feeling a sense of trepidation as we enter any and every interaction with another person, unsure of the land mines that await us.

Maybe you've already experienced this, even as you're navigating the mess of being a new Christian. Whether it's from the more established believers you're in relationship with or from friends and family who still don't get this whole Jesus thing, it's bound to happen, especially when a hot-button topic comes up. People talk, but they don't really talk. They make snide remarks about complex social issues and offer ad hominems against politicians and other public figures, but they don't really talk. To actually talk requires us to be able to listen, to learn, to empathize.

2. Coined by actor, author, and Internet pioneer Wil Wheaton, Wheaton's law is a simple four-word sentence: "Don't be a d—k." Yes, the bar is incredibly low.

To be willing to disagree, and to be willing to be wrong. In other words, to really talk requires humility. Humility is something that runs in short supply, even among Christians (sorry).

BITING, DEVOURING, AND BEING DUMMIES

Take Emily and me, for example. We rarely fight about anything of consequence. Not money, big parenting issues, or any of the stuff that is typically what you would think married people would fight about. For us, it's all about the details of old TV shows, minor household items, where to eat dinner on date night, and other assorted nonsense. So, we've gotten into the habit of saying things like, "Hey, let's keep fighting about this since it's really important," to clue us in that we're being kind of dumb. Because otherwise, all we were doing was trying to be the rightest person in the room, which means that, even when you win, you lose.

Because pride always loses (1 Peter 5:5; Proverbs 3:34).

In its most basic sense, pride is thinking of yourself *wrongly*. There are two ways this plays out. Typically, pride shows itself as thinking of yourself too highly. The know-it-all, "well, actually" guy who is determined to be the rightest person in the room, no matter what evidence is presented to the contrary.

That's where most of us live when it comes to pride. It's where I lived for a while as a newer Christian, especially as I started to develop doctrinal convictions. But truth be told, I wasn't exactly humble before that. I was the "sleeps in class, gets an A," "forgets to do a project, makes it up the night after it's due, and *still* gets the best grade" guy. In other words, *insufferable*. As my convictions became clearer, and especially as I started reading more books by Very Smart Guys™ (big books of theology, with nearly as many footnotes as letters behind their authors' names), the problem increased. My thoughts needed to be shared, and I was certain everything I believed was biblical and clearly in the text. But I had a problem: when I opened my mouth, my words were about as loving as hitting someone in the face with a hammer. I didn't know how to hear other points of view and frankly, didn't care that much. I wasn't a good listener because I didn't think I really needed to listen to anyone I disagreed with. I was excited about what I believed, but pride was getting in the way. Because I was prideful, I was too blind to see where other points of view had merit, or even when I was right in what I saw, I didn't know how to be discerning and graceful. I had a lot in common with those Paul warns about in Galatians 5:15, those who are so busy biting and devouring one another that they consume one another. (Maybe you can relate.)

The other way pride shows itself is a bit less commonly identified as such. Rather than thinking of yourself too highly, you think far too little of yourself. When someone recognizes your positive traits, a helpful insight, or even how God is at work in your life, you dismiss or deflect it. *They can't possibly be right,* you think. *Don't they know I'm nothing special?* No matter what another person says about *you,* they're wrong because *you* know better. (How arrogant is that?) This version of pride feels a little safer and, for a lot of Christians, is their default overcorrection to a puffed-up, overinflated sense of our own importance. Because we were wrong in one way, we must be wrong in *every* way. (Which also means we might also be wrong about being wrong about everything, but sometimes it takes a bit of time to figure that out.)

EMBRACING TWO LOST VIRTUES

In the last chapter, I said that character is the most important thing about a leader. Well, that's true of all of us. It's why pride is such a massive problem. Pride blinds us to certain realities—especially the reality that it's possible to be right and also wrong. That there is a way to disagree with one another while treating one another with respect and dignity. But to do it, we need to embrace two seemingly lost but related virtues.

1. Humility. If pride is thinking of yourself wrongly, humility is thinking of yourself correctly. Humility recognizes both your strengths and weaknesses simultaneously. The humble person doesn't downplay the unique ways they've been wired and gifted by God any more than they gloss over the particular ways they're tempted to sin. But more importantly, true humility doesn't cause us to think of ourselves much at all. Instead, it's others we consider as being more important than ourselves (Philippians 2:3). This is the point that Paul is making in Philippians 2 when he encourages having the same mind, or attitude, as Jesus, who,

> existing in the form of God,
> did not consider equality with God
> as something to be exploited.
> Instead he emptied himself
> by assuming the form of a servant,
> taking on the likeness of humanity.
> And when he had come as a man,
> he humbled himself by becoming obedient
> to the point of death—
> even to death on a cross. (Philippians 2:6–8)

Jesus showed us what true humility looked like, setting aside all the glory and honor he legitimately deserves to become one of us in order to live and die for us. So we want to become humble like this. We want God to help us to grow in our humility, so much so that we're not even thinking about humility because we're not thinking about ourselves at all.[3]

2. Tolerance. This second virtue was once prized by the Western world, but today it seems to be anything but. Without a doubt, you've heard this word, but you probably don't really know what it means because it's been twisted into meaning something it cannot. Traditionally, tolerance has meant that conflicting ideas and beliefs can coexist within society and that a diversity of views can contribute to a greater societal whole. You can respectfully disagree but still be at peace with your neighbors. But that's not what it means now. Tolerance is more commonly interpreted as a requirement to celebrate the views of others, even if you disagree with them.[4] Disagreement is intolerance, and intolerance will not be tolerated.

THE SECRET OF DISAGREEING
LIKE A CHRISTIAN

But you're a Christian now. You can't celebrate everything any more than you can reject everything. Whether we're talking about things like our views on human sexuality, political ideology, or generally irrelevant things such as TV shows, everything around you presents opportunities to find common ground or invites necessary disagreement. So how do we do that?

The secret to disagreeing like a Christian is best described as *convictional kindness*. Convictional kindness means having

---

3. This is a paraphrase of C. S. Lewis, who writes that "a really humble man ... will not be thinking about humility: he will not be thinking about himself at all." See Lewis, *Mere Christianity* (New York: HarperOne, 2001), 128.
4. This is why Christians who believe that God created human beings to be male and female, and that any sexual activity outside heterosexual marriage goes against God's design for us, are often called intolerant or bigots. But we disagree about what best leads to human flourishing, and those are two very different things.

a firm belief or opinion while also being willing to genuinely listen to the views and perspectives of others. It is the natural outworking of both humility and tolerance, and in another time this would have been called by another name: charity. Charity is the third lost virtue of our culture, one that disappeared as rapidly as our love of hot takes appeared, but has long been valued, especially by Christians. It is the sort of love that Paul wrote about as being patient and kind: "Love does not envy, is not boastful, is not arrogant, is not rude, is not self-seeking, is not irritable, and does not keep a record of wrongs. Love finds no joy in unrighteousness but rejoices in the truth. It bears all things, believes all things, hopes all things, endures all things" (1 Corinthians 13:4–7).

So how do we develop this kind of love for others? How do we develop the sort of convictional kindness, the charitable spirit, that allows us to engage in difficult discussions in a way that reflects Jesus?

Conviction. To be convictionally kind or charitable, you need to have convictions. These are the essentials that you hold to in your life and your faith, the matters you can't really leave unchallenged. This list should be pretty small (because if everything is essential, then *nothing* is essential). From a faith standpoint, these are the fundamentals, the things that, if you deny or reject them, you cannot honestly call yourself a Christian. That's why I spent so much time talking about those core habits for growing your faith at the beginning of this book. Your core convictions should come from your time reading the Bible, your prayer life, and your experience in a Christian community. Our core beliefs are found in the Bible, we pray that God will help us to see them, and we live them together as a church.

A second place to look to begin to get a grasp on the essentials of the Christian faith is the early creeds, which are summaries of these truths. The Apostles' Creed, for example, has been used for eighteen hundred years by Christians of many different backgrounds. The Nicene Creed is another one that beautifully focuses us on the essentials. Depending on your church's tradition and denomination, there may be confessional statement or a catechism (teaching guide) used to teach these truths, such as the Heidelberg or Westminster Catechism.[5]

Now, you'll notice that I'm only talking about your beliefs related to your faith here. That's because those are actually the easier ones to define. You're also going to develop secondary convictions, which have more to do about how you live your life day-to-day. For example, what you choose to or not to eat is a matter of conviction, but it's not a universal truth. It's far more subjective. Same with how to approach big decisions in parenting and education. These are areas where there isn't necessarily a right or wrong answer, but there is a right or wrong answer for you.

In both instances, though, you need to know that developing your convictions takes time. They likely will not appear overnight or after the first time you've read the Bible. You'll have time when you start to come to a conclusion and realize you're wrong and will need to retrace your steps through the process to find where the error happened. You're going to believe that certain things are more important than they really are and others are less important than they really are. As you grow, your convictions will grow, reshape, and reform with you.

Curiosity. Curiosity is essential to developing convictions, because it's all about wanting to learn and discover. There's a reason I wanted you to be thinking about how you engage with pop culture, books, and music a few chapters back. It's not just

5. All of these are easy to find online.

because art and creativity are good gifts from God (though they are). It's because when we explore different books, movies, music, and everything else we can think of, that exploration feeds our curiosity. Don't limit yourself to one school of thought; explore widely. Ask more established Christian friends to recommend good books to read. Learn from multiple perspectives—even if you're pretty sure you're going to disagree. It makes us better listeners and helps us to understand different points of view, especially as we are trying to live as Christians with the people who knew us before we believed the gospel.

Discernment. Discernment, at its most basic, is the ability to judge well. It is to, with reasonable accuracy, perceive the direction of certain lines of thought or to assess the character of an individual. Discernment goes hand in hand with curiosity and conviction. Uncritical curiosity, uncoupled from both conviction and discernment, will lead us to swing wildly from one extreme on every spectrum to another. The disillusioned political progressive becomes a rabid political populist; the disappointed legalist turns to licentiousness.[6]

Discernment requires us to be thoughtful, to ask good questions of everything we explore. In fact, go back and look at those questions I encouraged you to ask of art and pop culture in chapter 4. They don't just apply to books and movies. They apply to all of life. Every message needs to be explored in this way. Every concept is worthy of consideration in light of what we know about God and his world from the Bible, to see how it shapes our love for God and the people he made.

Developing your convictions, embracing curiosity, and practicing discernment is how we develop the kind of love Paul talks

---

6. Licentiousness is the rejection of previously established rules and boundaries.

about in 1 Corinthians. The kind of love that is not boastful or rude, that doesn't seek its own way, that allows us to talk to people—to *really* talk to them—without just trying to figure out the quickest route to being the rightest person in the room.

PUTTING CONVICTIONAL
KINDNESS INTO PRACTICE

Becoming convictionally kind means, first, becoming a good listener. But this doesn't *just* mean not talking over another person (although it does mean that). It means trying to understand what someone else is saying. To be a good listener means you need to ask good questions. In many cases, our disagreements aren't disagreements over essential matters—they're points at which we're talking past one another (this is especially true in political conversations). I might say one thing, but you won't hear it the way I mean because we're using similar language to mean different things. To address that, you need to ask questions instead of making assumptions about what someone else means.

A good question can diffuse a tense situation and help you potentially gain clarity, if not agreement. A really great question to ask in these moments is, "Can you help me understand what you mean by <statement or phrase>?" This can be a helpful signal to your discussion partner that you're entirely on the same page and potentially lead to more fruitful discussion as you go. Another worthy question to ask is, "What I heard you say is <summarize what you heard as best you can>. Am I understanding you correctly?" This gives your conversation partner the opportunity to either confirm or clarify what he or she means.

When you make it your aim to be a good listener, sometimes something incredible happens: you might find out you're wrong! It's not a guarantee that we are on the side of rightness in every disagreement. When this happens, don't get angry. Instead, treat it as a gift: it's an opportunity to grow in humility.

Second, respect your conscience (and that of others). Sometimes disagreements have nothing to do with any sort of essential conviction. In those cases, our role is to treat others' consciences with respect (Romans 14). We don't judge one another or argue over disputable matters. Instead, we exercise charity.

One big issue that's sure to come up for you is alcohol. Many Christians, particularly those from Baptist traditions, view drinking alcohol—even in moderation—as a sin. It is a view based in more in pragmatism than in biblical command, since you can't find any prohibitions against alcohol in the Bible. In some circles, people will argue that Jesus didn't make wine at the wedding in Cana; rather, he made grape juice (John 2:1–13). In attempting to avoid one sin, they in effect commit a far more serious one—adding to Scripture. While you should challenge this more serious error, you can do so without encouraging them to violate their convictions about consuming alcohol themselves. Instead, you can simply choose to not drink in their presence; you can also share your perspective from Scripture (assuming you've got one at this point).[7]

Third, you can agree to disagree. As a good listener and a respecter of consciences, it's important to also know that you don't have to agree with everyone on everything, and that's okay. You don't need to agree on everything in order to enjoy a productive discussion and a healthy relationship.

Fourth, don't engage. Sometimes the most charitable thing to do is not engage at all. This is the approach to take with people who you see are always looking for a fight. They love to argue and debate, not because they want to help anyone. They just

7. The Bible does not discourage drinking alcohol, but it encourages the use of wisdom. So if you choose to drink, do so in moderation. In other words, drink without getting drunk (see Romans 13:13; Galatians 5:21).

want to puff themselves up by being right. Titus 3:9–11 warns us against such things. "But avoid foolish debates, genealogies, quarrels, and disputes about the law, because they are unprofitable and worthless," Paul writes. "Reject a divisive person after a first and second warning. For you know that such a person has gone astray and is sinning; he is self-condemned." Divisive people, people who love controversy, should be warned about their behavior. It doesn't matter whether they're well respected within your church, or whether they're a Christian celebrity in their own mind on social media. They should be warned when what they are saying is false or when the way in which they are saying it doesn't reflect Christian love and charity. If divisive people persist in being divisive, have nothing to do with them. Don't engage the discussion. Walk away.

Finally, pray. Whenever you are invited into a potentially difficult or divisive discussion, it's always best to pray. Ask the Holy Spirit to give you clarity in understanding and the words you need to speak. Pray that everyone would hear well, that humility would be evident, and that love would reign in every moment.

That is how you practice convictional kindness. It's what it means to disagree like a Christian, with love that bears all things, believes all things, and hopes for all things—even in the midst of disagreement. It's a big task. You will step on more than one land mine throughout your life. But I can tell you from experience that any pain you feel as you grow in both conviction and kindness is worth it.

9

TRUE FAITH

//

TELL THE STORY THAT'S YOURS

Several years ago, one of my pastors texted me. A family situation had come up, and he needed someone to cover for him in leading the baptism class that weekend—could I help? I'd barely said yes before I was reading the teaching outline and materials. It was more or less what I expected to see in terms of the church's views on baptism: believers are to be baptized upon their confession of faith and be fully immersed in water as a symbol of the forgiveness of sins and new life they have because of Jesus. No great surprise there.

Then I got to the section designed to help people share their story of coming to faith. To help assist people with communicating, they were asked to speak to the following three points:

- What their lives were like before becoming Christians?

- What drew them to Jesus?

- What their lives were like now as believers?

Again, nothing controversial. In fact, I'm pretty certain that, with rare exception, the majority of Christians could effectively use this template to share their story of coming to faith. But as I started thinking about the template and listening to their stories, I kept hearing essentially the same story:

> Before I was a Christian, my life was a mess. I was living for myself, joyful on the outside but empty on the inside, numbing my insecurities with drugs, alcohol, and/or sex with random strangers. One night, things reached a breaking point—I hit rock bottom—and I gave my life to Jesus. After that, I realized I'd found what I'd been looking for, and now I'm living my life for him, serving in my church, and found an extra five dollars in my coat this morning.

The problem was, this wasn't my experience at all.

GOD'S UNIVERSAL AND UNIQUE GRACE

For many people, the templated story is entirely true, both in content and in form. They felt some kind of emptiness, a lacking in their lives. They had an obvious crisis moment. They came to faith in Jesus as a result, and their lives have changed for the better in clear ways. I love when this happens. I am thankful that God saves people in this way. But there are other stories too—stories that don't quite fit the neat and tidy template in the way that you might expect.

The second chapter of Ephesians spends a great deal of time unpacking the nature of salvation and how the gospel transforms us from being dead in our sins to being alive in Christ. The how of it comes down to one thing: we are saved by grace through faith (Ephesians 2:10). Everyone who is a Christian is saved in this way—God's grace, his unmerited, undeserved favor, given to all who put their faith in Jesus. While this how is true of all Christians at all times in all places, there is also a very personal aspect to this, something only you have experienced. It's God's grace in leading you to see that you needed Jesus to save you at all. God cares about you and not just in a general sense of having mapped out your overall direction and providing for your needs the way he does for everyone (Matthew 6:25–34). He is deeply, intimately invested in the minutiae, the tiniest, most obscure details of who you are; he planned each moment as he knitted you together in the womb (Psalm 139:13–14). Every moment of your life, from your first breath until you realized you needed Jesus to save you, was leading to that moment. Even though you and I didn't grow up with any understanding—or care for, for that matter—of God's existence, he cared for us. Though we likely did not give a moment of thought to life with God, he thinks deeply about every aspect of our lives.

The things you don't even think to think about are incredibly important to God.

By its very nature, grace of this sort cannot be templated, because it is the way God acted to save you specifically. Your experience is going to be distinct from all others, even if the ultimate means of your salvation are identical. It is too personal to be turned into a script. But that doesn't mean that it can't be shared.

DETEMPLATING GRACE

I realized this not long after becoming a Christian in fall 2006. I was in Honduras on my first overseas trip with a group from my church. Our leader asked me to tell the story of how I became a Christian to a group of teens from the Tegucigalpa area—through a *translator*. Despite not being comfortable speaking to a large group (or any size of group at the time), I agreed. But I didn't know how to tell the story in a way that would make sense— or at least wouldn't have them thinking I was crazy. I listened as others on my team shared how Jesus saved them, and sure enough, they used that basic three-point summary. Being new to all this, I tried to fit my experience into that outline. When my time came, I muddled my way through, but what I said, while not untrue, didn't feel *right*.

It was because my story didn't fit the template, and I was trying to force it in, as if it were a puzzle piece turned the wrong direction. I didn't feel any particular spiritual emptiness or lack of fulfillment prior to becoming a Christian. In fact, my life seemed to be going great. I was in a long-term relationship. I'd bought my first house. I had a decent-paying job. I was, by all accounts, happy. But in God's unique grace to me, the house I bought was a two-block walk from the Christian bookstore where I bought my first Bible—the Bible I only purchased to make fun of my friend Adam, the same friend who invited me to a ten-week evangelistic program that I slept through.

But that doesn't fit into the traditional crisis-point narrative because a crisis didn't show up until after I started reading the Bible and being drawn in by Jesus. But that doesn't fit the kind of mindset that we have in Western culture, which tends to default to an internal sort of conviction—an awareness of my sin (that wasn't present). I felt *fine*, even though I really wasn't. My awareness of my sins against God, my need for his forgiveness, came as I asked Jesus to save me, in the moment, not before, in a very Nathan-confronting-David sort of way (see 2 Samuel 11–12 for the whole story).[1] Conviction came from the *outside*, not from an internal awareness. But like I said, that doesn't quite fit the template.

---

1. David had Bathsheba brought to him, had sex with her, and then sent her away. When she discovered she was pregnant, he tried to buy off her husband, Uriah, and then killed him. At no time in the narrative is there any indication of a guilty conscience—not until Nathan the prophet comes and shames him with his parable of a rich man killing and eating a poor man's beloved lamb. A thoughtful book that explores how our culture affects how we read the Bible is Brandon J. O'Brien and E. Randolph Richards, *Misreading Scripture with Western Eyes* (Downers Grove, IL: IVP Academic, 2012).

What happened after doesn't fit it either. It was after Emily and I asked Jesus to save us—and he did—that we started to see the real crisis moments. Our lives turned into a giant mess. You've already read about a lot of it, from figuring out the basic mechanics of the Christian life to realizing that we shouldn't be living and sleeping together. But there was more: our newfound faith immediately put us in the middle of family conflict when we started to make rules around what activities were permissible in our home (if sex was off limits for us until we were married, we thought it needed to be off limits in the house, period). My new convictions led to difficulty at work because there were projects I was no longer comfortable working on. After our first daughter was born, the financial difficulties came. Then—well, I think you get the idea.

I'm sure someone more creative could spin my story to fit the template a bit more closely, but that's the problem: it would be spin. Had I not gone to the ten-week evangelism program, had I never gotten it into my head that the best way to make fun of my friend was to read the Bible, and had I never walked down the street to the Christian bookstore, there would have been no crisis. No family drama, no major work conflicts, possibly no financial issues. And I almost certainly wouldn't have been picked up out of my bed by a demon (I hope).

WHY TELL YOUR STORY AT ALL?

Whether it resembles the traditional three-point narrative or it feels more like a film where you're not entirely sure what's happening but you can't stop watching, your story is meant to be shared. Both Christians and non-Christians need to hear your story. But why should either care?

Your story encourages other Christians. Some Christians can tend to feel very defeated when looking at the culture. The narrative is often one of failure and fear. Churches are closing.

Attendance is shrinking. More people than ever have no religious affiliation. But your story can remind them that not everything is bleak and hopeless. People still believe the gospel. People who don't know the gospel and didn't grow up in church can and will hear and believe. You are proof of that, and they need to know it. But it's not just encouragement that your story offers.

Your story can motivate other Christians to share the gospel with non-Christians. Sometimes established Christians care more about evangelism in theory than in practice. It is an area where we all, to varying degrees, fail to practice what we preach. But to hear the stories of people like us is a reminder—and potentially a convicting one—that God still saves people today and that they can (and should) tell others what Christ has done to save them from sin.

Your story helps non-Christian friends and family make sense of what they're seeing in your life. There will always be some who think you're just trying to be a better person, and some might misinterpret you as being judgmental or self-righteous. But for the most part, telling your story helps friends and family who don't know Jesus start to get a handle on what's happened to you and why you're so different.

Your story opens the door to sharing the gospel. Sharing your story isn't the same as sharing the gospel. Your story is how you came to believe the gospel and be saved through the gospel. But it's not the gospel. Only the gospel—the death and resurrection of Jesus for our sins—is the gospel. But your story can provide a natural opening to sharing the most important message about the most important person in the universe.

Your story creates a reaction. Even though your story isn't the gospel, it still creates a reaction, a response, within its hearers. They have to do *something* with it. Sometimes that something is to dismiss your experiences out of hand or to rationalize or explain it away. Sometimes the response is rejection. But your story may also cause its hearers to consider their own lives and evaluate their beliefs, perhaps for the very first time.

EXPECT UNEXPECTED REACTIONS

Both Emily and I are all too familiar with getting a reaction from our efforts to share the gospel as we've told our story. But those reactions are rarely what we expect.

Several years ago, when we were still brand-new Christians (and brand-new parents), Emily prayed for an opportunity to tell her parents about Jesus. She wanted (and still wants) them to put their faith in Jesus. As she prayed, she began to imagine a scene straight out of a very special episode of *Full House*, or some other cheesy sitcom from the 1980s. In this imaginary scenario, Emily and her mom were sitting at our house, enjoying a cup of tea at the dining table and having a conversation:

> Emily's mom: "Gee, honey, I've noticed some significant changes in you in the last several months. You're so different compared to how you were even a year ago. What happened?
>
> Emily: "Well, Mom, I became a Christian, and here's what happened and what that means …"

After boldly and clearly sharing the gospel with her, the imaginary scenario ended with Emily's mom then putting her faith in Jesus.

Then, sometime later, Emily's mom came over for tea with Emily. They sat down at the dining table and chatted for a while. Everything was just as she'd imagined, until her mom finally said, "Gee, honey, *Aaron's* really different. What happened?"

Not exactly what she imagined, but beggars can't be choosers, so Emily went for it. She told her mom what happened—why *I* was so different and how both she and I had become Christians.

A few days later, her mom emailed and shared how the discussion motivated her to start attending a Buddhist group in her town as a way to connect with her spiritual side. Which is not exactly the response one would hope to receive after sharing the gospel with a loved one.

But this isn't the only example. One couple, one-half of whom was the best man at our wedding, drifted away from us after we told them the story and shared the gospel with them. Some family members have made it clear that they are unwilling and uninterested in hearing—even engaging in any sort of discussion is a hard no. (We keep praying for those opportunities anyway.)

But it's not all been bad. When Emily was briefly on Twitter, an editor for a widely read magazine asked her to write her testimony and have it published. That led to fifteen minutes of Christian fame, where our family was put in the spotlight for two separate micro-documentaries that aired on a couple of talk shows on faith-based cable channels. Several hundred people, we were later told, called the show and shared that they made a profession of faith after watching our story.

None of this is what I would have expected. The chances are low that anything like it will ever happen again, at least to us. (I can't say what will happen to you.) But what I can say is this: you're going to have opportunities to share your story and to share the gospel as a result. Take advantage of every opportunity. Don't worry about how people will respond. Just be faithful and talk.

HOW DO YOU TELL YOUR STORY?

Contrary to the standard formula I first heard, there isn't a truly standard way to tell your story. Because we live in the real world, life doesn't neatly fall into a template. But that doesn't mean there aren't some guiding principles and practices to consider.

Share why you became interested in Jesus. Maybe you were in the midst of a crisis. Maybe you were studying and comparing different religions. Maybe you came across an interesting podcast. Maybe you wanted to make fun of Christians. Whatever the reason, why you became interested in Jesus in the first place really does matter. It helps people relate to your story. It gives them context for what led you to become a Christian and perhaps, to see what you first saw. So talk about it.

Talk about what led you to turn to Jesus. Whatever that was— whether it was the sudden onset of conviction from the Holy Spirit, a slow process of exploration, or anything in between— this is important, too. Why is Jesus interesting to you? What is it about him that would make you want to upend everything in your life like this?

Share the good and bad of becoming a Christian. Be honest about what it's like trying to figure out the mess. What challenges have you had along the way? What's different between life before and after? Acknowledge that there are questions you're still working through, and don't pretend you've got all the answers already.

Take your time. Don't try to rush through what happened to you. Give your story the room it needs to breathe. Be okay with rabbit trails. Be cool with tangents. Sometimes those are the details that stick the most.

Trust God with the rest. Don't worry about how people are going to respond. Don't expect those hearing your story to come to faith in that moment. It might not—I dare say, it probably won't—happen that way. It might be years down the road. It might be something you never get to see. But it's okay. Just be faithful to tell your story and trust God with doing whatever he's going to do with it.

There's nothing earth shattering here. That's the point. Telling your story isn't supposed to be difficult. Don't overthink it. Don't worry too much about being prepared. It's your life. You experienced it. The way God worked in your life will encourage a response from those who hear it, whether they're Christians or not and whether they go on to believe the gospel or not. So go ahead and talk.

10

MY HERO

//

THE KIND OF CHRISTIAN TO ASPIRE TO BE

What do you want to be when you grow up? This probably isn't a question you're used to being asked. After all, you *are* grown up. This is the sort of question you ask a child, expecting the answer to be a firefighter, doctor, rock star, or YouTuber. (I wanted to make comic books.) But don't forget what I said at the beginning of this book: you are a grown-up physically, but when it comes to your faith, you're still learning to walk.

So back to the question: What do you want to be when you grow up? Maybe there's a better way to put it:

What sort of Christian do you hope to be as you grow in your faith?

I've wrestled with this question for a long time. In fact, it wasn't until fairly recently that I even came to what I think is actually a reasonable and biblical answer. What has been much easier is trying to figure out the sort of Christian I don't want to be. Let me tell you about two of them.

THE CULTURE-WARRING CHRISTIAN

The first is the culture-warring Christian. While this mindset is not exclusive to one political or theological perspective, the most visible culture-warring Christians tend to be conservative men and women who see the devil around every corner.[1] The world is going to hell in a handbasket, they say, so it's time for Christians—especially *American* Christians—to stand up against a coming wave of persecution. What this sort of Christian gets right is that he or she recognizes that there are very real challenges to living faithfully all around us, threats we do legitimately need to confront as Christians. Christians *are* challenged to celebrate views and support practices that we cannot, typically issues related to sex and identity from outside the church and false teaching that damages our faith from inside the church.

However, the culture warrior rarely does much to counter these challenges in a way that reflects the gospel. Part of the reason for that is that culture warriors don't seem to know which fights to choose. Every fight seems to be treated as one worth having, if not starting. It could be defending a Christian business owner's right to choose whom they serve (which is a legitimate concern for both Christians and non-Christians alike). It could be declaring that there's a war on Christmas and saying "Happy Holidays" is a denial of Jesus's existence (which is nonsense). It could be upholding the value and dignity of human life, regardless of age, cognitive ability, ethnicity, or gender (again, legitimate concerns). Or it could be claiming that a toy brand updating its logo is a rejection of distinctions between genders (again, nonsense). The problem here is that, by taking a reactionary

---

1. There are an ever-increasing number of men and women on the extreme progressive or liberal end of both the theological and political spectrums who use the exact same tactics as their conservative counterparts.

I'M A CHRISTIAN—NOW WHAT?

approach, legitimate concerns are tuned out—they can't be heard amid the noise. The culture warriors simply escalate the battles, thus perpetuating the cycle. Every decision by a company, celebrity, or politician is or has the potential to be, The Greatest Threat to the Gospel in Our Time™, even if it's not.

Another problem with becoming a culture-warring Christian is the inconsistency in making distinctions between friends and (apparent) foes. Rather than having true friends, such Christians have factional ones, as David French describes them.[2] These are fragile relationships, where one person is considered their ally one moment and declared an enemy of the church the next, depending on the subject and whether they agree. Allies are not allies at all; they are allies of convenience. "The enemy of my enemy is my friend."

The final cause for concern is that the solutions to the culture wars proposed by culture-warring Christians have very little to do with the gospel itself, even as they give lip service to the gospel. Instead, the answers tend to be about wielding power, typically based on political affiliations. The answer to the threats we face lies in voting for a specific political party, in putting the right people in power—and often in accumulating power for ourselves. With those things, we can make a difference. If not, we'll call for a boycott of a business (until something we want enough goes on sale).

I don't think this is what Jude had in mind when he encouraged his readers to "contend for the faith" (Jude 3).

2. David French, "Lost Friendships Break Hearts and Nations," The French Press, July 11, 2011, https://frenchpress.thedispatch.com/p/lost-friendships-break-hearts-and.

THE CAPITULATING CHRISTIAN

If one error is to be a culture-warring Christian, always looking forward to a fight, the opposite error can be just as damaging. Let's call this one the capitulating Christian. The capitulating Christian recognizes the importance of what some might call a "winsome witness"—of showing genuine love to their neighbors in the world, regardless of their background, beliefs, or behaviors. This is a good and right desire because the Bible does tell us that Christians are supposed to be known for our love for one another, and we are commanded to love those who disagree with us—even those who outright hate us (John 13:35; Matthew 5:43–48). They see how the culture-warring Christian falls short of this ideal in how they demonize their opponents and want to avoid that. But that desire—itself not a bad one—tends to lead them to seek to avoid conflict with the world as a whole.

This approach tends to lead to downplaying or denying what makes Christianity genuinely unique in order to promote a superficial unity with the rest of the world. For example, because Christians believe that there really is only one God and that the only way to have our sins forgiven is through faith in Jesus—that he is the only way anyone, anywhere, in space, time, and history, is saved—we're in conflict with literally every other religion and belief system in the universe. This belief is either true or it isn't; it's not something we can agree to disagree on. But some capitulating Christians will attempt to downplay this, just as they will downplay what we believe about the Bible (and sometimes do so by accusing Christians of worshiping it) and our beliefs about sex, marriage, and gender.

But capitulation falls far short on every count. It is not loving to people who don't know Jesus, people like you and me before we believed, because it is dishonest about Christianity. In downplaying and denying the core truths of the faith, in trying to avoid the more complex and uncomfortable subjects, it welcomes sin and false teachers into the church, leading people away from the truth instead of toward it. Attempting to sand off the rough edges of Christianity doesn't make the idea of following Jesus more appealing; it's not following Jesus at all.

Neither the culture-warring Christian nor the capitulating Christian has much to offer the world. Neither represents Jesus the way he calls us to because both of them violate the commandments Jesus calls the greatest—"Love the Lord your God with all your heart, with all your soul, and with all your mind," and likewise "Love your neighbor as yourself" (Matthew 22:37, 39). All faithfulness to God—the entirety of his law—depends on these commands (Matthew 22:40). Culture warring violates the first commandment in its failure to trust God in all things. It violates the second in its demonizing of people made in God's image. Capitulation violates the first by failing to treat God with the respect and honor he is due. It violates the second by being both unloving and dishonest about God to people who don't know Jesus. So whatever else we aspire to be, it can't be either of these. So what is?

CORRECTING CULTURE WARRIORS
AND CAPITULATORS

My wife and I talk about this a lot. As Canadians living in the American South, we've got a front-row seat to the tug-of-war between culture warring and capitulation. It is pure madness; the outrage and posturing that go along with both are spiritually exhausting, so much so that Emily once asked, "Can't I just love Jesus and be a good neighbor?" If you're asking this, yes, you can. In fact, that's exactly what God wants us to do. It's the kind of Christian we're *supposed* to be, at least, if an apostle named Peter is to be believed.

Peter wrote two of the letters that are a part of the New Testament. The first of them, 1 Peter, speaks directly to this issue, as Peter encouraged and challenged a group of persecuted Christians—Christians who did not have any kind of cultural acceptance—to remain faithful. Even though there was no official policy against Christians at the time, these believers were often verbally abused, discriminated against, and sometimes harassed by local officials. They had no voice. They had no influence. They had no hope that things would get better. So what were they to do? Should they start fighting back—going to war against a culture that was hostile to them? Should they give up their distinctiveness and go along to get along? Peter told them to do neither. He challenged them to "be like-minded and sympathetic, love one another, and be compassionate and humble, not paying back evil for evil or insult for insult but, on the contrary, giving a blessing, since you were called for this, so that you may inherit a blessing" (1 Peter 3:8–9).

This passage is a direct challenge to the culture-warring mindset, so much so that it's tempting to subtitle it Rageaholics Anonymous. But if we did that, we'd miss the word to those tempted to capitulate, to self-censor and live in silence. This passage, and the one that follows, confronts both errors as Peter challenges his readers to focus on living harmoniously in humility—to live in unity, sympathy, love, and compassion.

If we are to live as Christians in the world, all of us need to keep Jesus at the center of our community and lives. He is the One we are all united to through faith (Ephesians 2:10; 3:17; 1 Corinthians 1:30; 2 Corinthians 13:5), and he is the One whom we are united together by (1 Corinthians 6:15). This is particularly challenging in times when we feel threatened because our fight-or-flight response kicks in. If we're fighters, we're likely to launch a counterattack against any real or perceived threat. If we're prone to flight, we're likely to do whatever we can to escape the discord that threats can bring our way. But, maintaining a focus on the gospel, we can remember that because of Jesus, even when we experience suffering, we don't have to respond by either fleeing or fighting. Instead, we hold steady in our love for God and love for our family in Jesus, being sympathetic to one another's experiences and showing compassion to those who are tempted to flee, those who are prone to fight, and those who are trying to discredit us. This sort of harmonious living, this like-mindedness, takes humility—it requires us to think of others more highly than ourselves, to put the needs and preferences of others ahead of our own.

What Peter describes is convictional kindness in practice—that same principle you learned about a couple of chapters ago. Convictional kindness calls us to live in harmony within the church and to reject the temptation to repay evil for evil. Convictional kindness keeps us focused on Jesus and allows us to be a blessing to the world through our conduct in it—even if that blessing is seen as a curse by those around us.[3] So Peter challenges all his readers—and us—to remember that if Jesus is who and what we're all about, then we can expect to experience conflict. We can't not, especially if so much of what the world says is good is opposed to God (which it is). When we defend the oppressed, when we speak up against evil, when we engage with the world to bless the world, we're going to be opposed. So we need to embrace this truth because it is better to "suffer for doing good, if that should be God's will, than for doing evil" (1 Peter 3:17).

When we do experience conflict because of our faith in Jesus, do you know what we're supposed to do? We don't need to run away, and we don't need to put our hope in people who will let us

---

3. In certain parts of the world, that is how Christians are seen, not least because of our insistence that there is one God who made us and has the right to tell us how we're meant to live.

down. Instead, Peter says, "Do not fear them or be intimidated, but in your hearts regard Christ the Lord as holy, ready at any time to give a defense to anyone who asks you for a reason for the hope that is in you" (1 Peter 3:14–15). To regard Christ as holy means to remember who he is—remember that he is God. He is the literal king of the universe, the One who came into this world as a human being, suffered, died, and rose again to save people like us. People who reject him, who put their trust in people and structures and pretend gods that will always let them down. The very kinds of people who insulted, demeaned, abused, and ultimately murdered him. And what did he do? He did not repay evil for evil. He did not respond in kind to those who mistreated him. Instead, He blessed them. He blessed us.

So when we think about how to respond to others—when we think about the kind of Christians we ought to be—that's what it comes down to. We remember Jesus, we focus on him, and when we eventually are disparaged for our faith, when we are given the side-eye, or called ignorant or bigots because of what we believe, we point to Jesus as the answer. We believe, and we don't stop believing, and we keep acting out of our belief because Jesus is real. He is God, and someday, either when we die or when he returns to this world, we will live with him forever (Revelation 22:3–5).

So, culture warring isn't the answer, and neither is capitulation. Convictional kindness is the answer. Because that's the answer, we can pursue the kind of life that Paul commends: "to seek to lead a quiet life, to mind your own business, and to work with your own hands, as we commanded you, so that you may behave properly in the presence of outsiders and not be dependent on anyone" (1 Thessalonians 4:11–12).

People like that are the kind of Christian you should want to be when you grow up.

MY HERO

131

HEROES YOU'VE NEVER HEARD OF
(AND LIKE IT THAT WAY)

If you ask a more established believer, someone who grew up in church, they will likely start talking about specific people who embody the ideal Christian. They're their personal heroes of the faith, like evangelist Billy Graham, great nineteenth-century preachers like D. L. Moody or Charles Spurgeon, the martyred missionary Jim Elliot, and dozens of others you've probably never heard of. All of us have these kinds of heroes—even Christians back when the New Testament was still being written did. Hebrews 11, for example, gives a list of examples from the Old Testament that focus on each person's faith, specifically how they recognized that Jesus was better than anything the world had to offer. Some, by faith, fought incredible battles. Some, by faith, had their children raised from the dead. Others still, by faith, endured terrible hardship and suffering. Of all these, the author writes, "The world was not worthy of them" (Hebrews 11:38).

That's the description that comes to mind when I think about those in my life who seek to live quiet lives, to mind their own business, and to do the work God's called them to do.

One of these is Ray, a retired pastor in his seventies. He is a man I don't get to spend nearly as much time with as I would like. (Most people who know him feel this way.) He's one of these men to whom you feel like you should be confessing everything you ever did. It's not because he's perfect. He'd undoubtedly tell you that he struggles with sin like the rest of us. But it's clear that he *knows* Jesus. I don't know how else to put it. It's the result of years of faithfully focusing on his relationship with Jesus as he studies the Bible, talks to God in prayer, and invests in people. Every time I have spent any time with him, it encourages me to do likewise.

Another is Steve, one of the elders at my church. He's a retired elementary school principal and now serves in a Christian counseling ministry. He's got a very laid-back, down-home, country demeanor that puts everyone he meets immediately at ease. He is rarely seen at the front of the room and prefers to avoid the spotlight. But he's always ready to listen, to pray, to open up his home to friends and strangers.

There are so many others, like Andrew and Cristal, Nathan and Jessica. Adam and Larissa, Michael and Ashley. C. A. and Terri, Dustin and Laurie Ann. Leo and Amanda, Clark and Anna. Mark and Pam, David and Sarah. There's nothing particularly special about any of them in the sense that none of them have any notoriety. None of them are known outside their communities, for the most part. They're regular people. But they seek to live quiet lives. They focus on what's in front of them—their families, their church, their jobs, and communities. For the most part, none of them could tell you what's happening in a different church or community, because it's not their business. They're too busy going about the work God's called them to. Because of it, they are people whom God's grace flows through as they love Jesus imperfectly day by day.

The world is not worthy of these sorts of people.

BECOMING THE KIND OF CHRISTIAN WE ASPIRE TO BE

That's the kind of Christian I aspire to be—a convictionally kind one. One who lives a quiet life, who isn't concerned about this-or-that controversy, but loves Jesus and loves the people in his church and community. I hope it's the kind you will aspire to be too. But how do you become this kind of Christian?

It's something that will take you a lifetime, but explaining it is pretty simple. In fact, it's what I've been talking to you about throughout this whole book and what I hope your church is helping you to do at this very moment. To become a convictionally kind Christian, you need to build the core habits, the spiritual disciplines, of the Christian life:

- To regularly read the Bible, with Jesus as the hero of its story.

- To pray consistently, talking to the God who loves you and is intimately involved *and* interested in all the details of your life.

- To be a part of a community of Christians where you know them deeply, and they deeply know you.

These three provide the foundation and framework for your growth in your faith. Everything else I've talked with you about in this book is built on those three. The Bible is the source of our convictions about our faith, and the standard to which we hold ourselves. Prayer is how we develop our relationship with God. Christian community is where we all find help in worshiping Jesus together as we seek the good of one another, our communities, and the world.

It's going to be messy. You'll run afoul of other peoples' convictions, just as they will run afoul of yours. You'll be disappointed by decisions you made and ones you wish you had. You'll find that what you hoped would be a straight walk toward maturity is more like staggering, crawling, and rolling your way toward holiness, like the pirate Yellowbeard trying to remember the way to his treasure.[4] But through the good and bad you experience, whether in times of joy or sorrow, you will endure. Your endurance will produce your character. Your character will produce hope. And this hope will never disappoint, "because

---

4. While I don't encourage watching the film for multiple content reasons, *Yellowbeard* (1983) really does give the best visual representation of this path. And despite claims that Jack Sparrow was an homage to Keith Richards of the Rolling Stones, I think Johnny Depp was totally riffing off Graham Chapman, who played the titular pirate.

God's love has been poured out in our hearts through the Holy Spirit who was given to us" (Romans 5:3–5).

Therefore, as you close this book, let me encourage you one last time: Seek to live a quiet life. Focus on where God has placed you and the work he has called you to in this moment. Pursue a heart of convictional kindness. Put all your hope in Jesus, the author and finisher of your faith (Hebrews 12:2). He will never disappoint.

A PASTORAL POSTSCRIPT
FOR DISCIPLE MAKERS

In 2016, I experienced a new kind of culture shock: I moved. Now, I moved a lot as a kid and moved regularly as an adult too. I moved cross-country twice, even. But this move was different. I moved from my home country—Canada—to the United States. And not just to the United States but to Tennessee. To the *South*, right in the heart of the Bible Belt. Flannery O'Connor, a Southern Gothic storyteller, describes the South as hardly being Christ-centered, but "most certainly Christ-haunted."[1] There is less of a certainty or conviction that Christianity is true and more of a fear that it may be. So a Christian wallpaper, a thin veneer of religiosity, covers up all the crud that is out in the open in a post- or pre-Christian culture. People might go to church but they don't necessarily believe the gospel.

It's in this context that I've been asked on more than one occasion the question that hurts my soul more than almost any other: "Should churches even try to make adult converts?" It is a fair one, especially if your context is one where growing up in a culture where Christianity seems normal. If most people who

---

1. Flannery O'Connor and Sally Fitzgerald, *Mystery and Manners: Occasional Prose* (New York: Farrar, Straus & Giroux, 1969), 44–45.

are a part of your church have always been part of a church and grew up in families that love Jesus, the idea of someone who has no idea about anything to do with Christianity is unfathomable, and it's easier to believe they should be less of a priority in your mission efforts.

If this is your situation, I'm willing to bet that you had trouble with some of what I shared in this book, whether it was the experiences I described or the advice I offered. That's okay because it's not meant for you. But it is meant for the people I believe you will increasingly be serving—and serving alongside—in the years to come.

YOUR CURRENT (AND COMING) MISSION FIELD

You've undoubtedly heard the term "post-Christian" used to refer to Canada, the UK, and other Western nations, along with parts of the United States. It's easiest to think of a post-Christian culture as the result of culture shifting from values informed by a historic connection to the Christian faith to something else. Post-Christian cultures tend to have a faulty memory of Christian values; to many within those cultures, Christian values, and Christianity with it, are limiting and oppressive—they keep you from your true self. As a result, Christianity is typically met with hostility.

But what happens when the faulty memory fades entirely, maybe a generation or two after post-Christianity? Hostility gives way to ignorance. People in these cultures won't see Christianity positively or negatively. They won't necessarily think Christianity is oppressive because they won't think about it at all.

This is where I believe we already are in many parts of the Western world. It's certainly true of many major cities in Canada. Toronto, London, and Montreal, despite there being several large churches in each of these cities, aren't so much post-Christian as they are beyond it, in something almost like a pre-Christian culture. I say almost because it's not quite the same a true pre-Christian culture, where the gospel has never been heard before, which is the sort of culture where the gospel spread like wildfire in the first century. The West cannot become truly pre-Christian because Christianity's influence is so deeply ingrained into virtually every facet of Western society, even if there is no longer awareness of it. Our laws, our collective morality, our pursuit of the common good—all of it stems from Christianity's influence.

The same will happen in the United States as well. In some regions, we're already there, where others, like the Bible Belt, are seeing the last vestiges of cultural Christianity fall away.[2] But however you want to label it, whether post-Christian or post-post-/almost pre-Christian, this cultural moment offers a different set of challenges to you as disciple makers and as witnesses to the gospel. You are increasingly serving people without the history you might think they have and with practical issues that you inevitably will feel unequipped to deal with effectively. Some of them might seem silly to you; some will make you break out into a cold sweat. But this is the world in which you live. This is the world in which God has placed you to fulfill his mission.

SEVEN QUESTIONS TO NAVIGATE THE MESS WITH ADULT NEW BELIEVERS

If you're faithfully pursuing the calling God gives his church, to make disciples of every people group and culture (Matthew 28:18–20), then, increasingly, you should expect adults coming

2. Kristy Etheridge, "The Vanishing Bible Belt: The Secrets Southern Churches Must Learn to Stay Healthy," Lifeway Research, February 3, 2021, https://research.lifeway.com/2021/02/03/the-vanishing-bible-belt-the-secrets-southern-churches-must-learn-to-stay-healthy.

to faith to be the norm. Conversion won't and can't come solely from the children of believers coming to faith. God shows no partiality in this way. Because adults are going to come to faith, it means that discipleship is going to be messier than what you might be used to.

As a man who came to faith as an adult, my goal in writing this book isn't only to help people like me navigate the mess of coming to faith. I want to help *you* help them, too. To do that, I want to offer some guidance by posing seven questions you should be asking as you consider discipling these new Christians.

1. HOW CAN MY CHURCH HELP NEW BELIEVERS DEVELOP A HABIT OF REGULAR BIBLE READING?

At the beginning of this book, I shared three core habits, or disciplines, that form the foundation of the Christian life. The first of these is developing a lifelong habit of reading the Bible. Here's how you and your church can help those who come to faith as adults:

Don't assume they have a Bible. It's good to have the practice on Sundays of encouraging people to open their Bibles. But you would do well to always have several giveaway copies handy, either in the pockets of a pew (if your church has those), underneath seats, or on a table in your meeting space. If you really want to help people appreciate it, try to get some nice ones. Publishers usually offer bulk purchase discounts on their Bibles, so it shouldn't break the bank. It's also a good way to engage your congregation to serve these new believers by asking them contribute to the purchase.

Teach them how to study it. Many of the more established believers in your church don't read the Bible as often as they know they should because they don't feel confident that they can understand it. And if people who've been in churches for years don't feel confident, how do you think a new believer will feel? So teach them the basics of Bible study using a system like the Seven Arrows of Bible Study.[3] Walk through an accessible introduction to interpretive principles like *Knowing Scripture* by R. C. Sproul.

Practice what you preach. I've been present when pastors expressed how desperate they were for people to read their Bibles, but the Bible itself was only minimally present in their ministries. So, if you believe the Bible is important, then make sure it's the core of all your teaching ministries, from children's ministry all the way through to the pulpit. If it's important to you, it will be important to the congregation.

Share what your Bible reading plans and practices look like. Share how you read the Bible and invite people to read with you. Let them learn from your life as well as your teaching.

2. HOW CAN MY CHURCH HELP NEW BELIEVERS DEVELOP A LIFELONG HABIT OF PRAYER?

Prayer is the second of the three core habits that shape the Christian life and is something that, with rare exception, it seems as though we all struggle with. Helping a new believer develop a lifelong habit of prayer is easier and harder than you might think. To help, here are three things I would encourage:

Consider the language you use in prayer. When you pray, does it sound like you? Do your prayers sound like you talk? Are they overly formal and King James-y? If there is a marked difference between how you speak regularly and how you pray, then it may create an unnecessary barrier to new believers. Prayer is, first and foremost, talking to God. There is no special separate vocabulary required.

---

3. Matt Rogers, "The Seven Arrows of Bible Reading," The Gospel Project, August 4, 2021, https://gospelproject.lifeway.com/7-arrows-of-bible-reading/.

Share what your prayer life looks like. Share the techniques you use to maintain your prayer life. Do you have a calendar reminder? Do you use a journal? Just like with reading the Bible, new believers will benefit from your example of a healthy prayer life at least as much as, if not more than, your instruction.

Talk about the ways you've seen God answer prayers. Part of the reason people struggle with prayer is they wonder whether it really works. Sharing the ways you have seen God answer your prayers is a meaningful way to encourage others to see the value of prayer and encourage them to keep praying (even when it's hard).

3. HOW CAN MY CHURCH BE A HEALTHY PLACE FOR NEW BELIEVERS?

For your church to be a healthy place for new believers means it needs to be a healthy place for all people. The signs of a healthy church in chapter 3 are a great starting point for your consideration, but I would also challenge you to look at how those reflect your actual practice:

If you're a pastor, are you a part of the congregation? Before service, are you worshiping with the congregation, or are you in a greenroom? Are you in a community group—specifically, one you don't lead? Do you have friends in your congregation? If your answer to the majority of these questions is no, then it might be that your church may not even be a safe place for you. If it's not a safe place for you, how can it be a safe place for anyone else?

How do you handle sin in your church? Does all sin get taken seriously in practice, or are there only some sins that matter? A church that doesn't deal with sin biblically isn't a safe place, which means that people will always be hiding something.

Do people in the congregation feel safe to ask questions? This is one of the clearest signs of the health of your church. If people ask questions, whether about doctrine or about church practices, it's not a sign of disrespect or disagreement. Most of the time, they just want to understand better what we believe or what we do. So let them ask. Encourage them to ask. When they do, give an answer. It doesn't matter if it's about church finances, something they heard in a sermon, or on your views about the second coming; they should be able to expect an answer.

4. HOW CAN MY CHURCH HELP NEW BELIEVERS EMBRACE CREATIVITY IN A CHRIST-HONORING WAY?

Many established Christians struggle in this area, especially those who've been raised in church cultures where the response to secular entertainment organizations acting like secular entertainment organizations is to boycott them and then make entertainment material that's kind of like theirs (just not as good). Instead, here's what I would encourage:

Calibrate your convictions. You need to honor your convictions because to violate them is always to sin (Romans 14:1–5). However, your convictions may also require calibration. This means that you need to make sure that your convictions aren't based simply in your cultural norms but rooted in the Bible itself. This is not easy; in fact, it will take a lot of time, prayer, and humility as you explore the difference between the two through reading, discussion, and putting your convictions into practice. But you need to do this work, both for your church and for yourself, lest you impose your convictions on others in a way that violates their own.

Reject simplistic substitutes. The answer to embracing creativity in any form is not to offer a knock-off or a sound-alike. We shouldn't encourage people to watch the "best Christian movie"— we should encourage them to watch objectively great movies (as subjective as that statement may be). Substitute creativity is mediocrity, and when it comes to creativity, mediocrity is a sin.

Encourage and develop discernment. There are certain things that must always be rejected outright, such as any form of creativity that demeans and denigrates human beings (pornographic material is the most obvious example, but it's not the only content of this sort). However, the majority of creative content, whether books, movies, or music, doesn't necessarily need to be rejected as much as have discernment applied. Help new believers consider the operating assumptions of what they see, hear, and read. Encourage them to examine how a form of creativity aligns with the truth of Scripture, how it deviates, and how it helps them love God more.

5. HOW CAN MY CHURCH SUPPORT NEW BELIEVERS AS THEY PURSUE SEXUAL PURITY?

In chapter 5, you read about how Emily and I became Christians while cohabitating. That was the first and most significant challenge that we faced coming to faith because we didn't even know it was an issue until a couple of months later when God convicted us.

Our solution, the one worked out with our pastor, was not ideal. It was a concession. But even so, God showed immense kindness to us and to our church as we worked through the problem. New Christians today might be in even more complicated situations, some that would make ours seem easy by comparison. It's possible, even likely, that children are in the mix, to say nothing of the possibility of being involved in a same-sex relationship (which necessarily involves the permanent end of the relationship).

When it comes to heterosexual relationships, if children are involved, then an expedient marriage combined with a great deal of family counseling is often the right solution. Children flourish when both parents are present in a healthy and functional relationship, so we are right to encourage this. So, in your church, you can help them by providing counseling—and it needs to be more than simply pastoral (though that also is necessary). Family dynamics will be in upheaval when one or both adults come to faith, so it's important that we care for the entire family and not assume the issue is addressed after the husband and wife say "I do."

It isn't less complicated for couples without children. For these, the best solution for the vast majority is to have a couple live apart as they either work toward marriage or determine whether the relationship should even continue at all. (And it should be said that if one remains committed to *not* following Jesus, then the relationship should end.) I don't believe getting married right away is necessarily the best solution for most couples in this situation because there is so much deprogramming that needs to happen. They have to relearn the appropriate boundaries of relationships, how men and women are meant to interact both inside and outside marriage, and, of course, what marriage means altogether. We need to recognize and honor the complexity of the situation they're in. This is one of the areas where churches tend to fall short and an error I want you to avoid. Don't just *tell* adult new believers to separate and work toward marriage. Help them. Do the work. If God has brought them to your church, you're called to work with them to figure out *how* to make the situation work in the way God will get the most glory. If you're serious about them living apart, make sure there's a way for that to happen. For example:

- Does anyone in the congregation have a guest room that can be offered as a place for one member of the couple to live?

- Is there another single Christian of the same gender who could move in and take over the rent or mortgage obligation of the opposite-gender member of the relationship while that person moves out?

- Can the church absorb or subsidize the cost of housing to allow the couple to live faithfully in the interim between coming to faith and getting married?

Discipling through these situations means you're going to have to do more than just tell people what they should do. You need to step into the mess with them and lead them out. This will require a significant investment of time and, yes, resources, but believe me, it will be worth it.

6. HOW DOES MY CHURCH HELP NEW BELIEVERS DEVELOP THE CHARACTER AND MATURITY TO SOMEDAY LEAD?

Western culture—including Western church culture—and the Bible are often at odds on this point. Western churches tend to place a premium on skills and gifts rather than on maturity and character. But according to the Bible, it doesn't matter how skilled someone might be in certain areas; if they're a new convert, they are not fit to lead. Period. Putting a person in a leadership role before they're ready can be disastrous. If you're not sure about that, consider the examples of Mark Driscoll, James MacDonald, Steven Furtick, and Bill Hybels. All were and are compelling speakers. All started leading relatively young. But their speaking abilities drastically outpaced their character, and not one of them fits the qualifications an elder according to 1 Timothy 3.

Now, you're probably not going to create monsters if you make the mistake of putting a new believer in a leadership role. But you'll still do a tremendous amount of damage. So rather than putting new believers in leadership roles too fast, here's what I would encourage:

Don't confuse excitement with maturity. When you see someone who is excited and eager, don't assume that they're qualified to lead. It could simply be that they're genuinely excited, and you're excited about their excitement because you're surrounded by apathy.

Have higher standards for volunteering and leadership. Another way to say this is to repent of the mirror test. If your measure of leadership is that people are excited, willing, and appear to be breathing, then you need higher standards. Focus on the qualities Scripture describes and look for people genuinely who exhibit these characteristics. The new believers among you, I guarantee, are not them, regardless of what they do in their nine-to-five.

Invest in your new believers. Take the time to get to know these men and women. Befriend them. Mentor them. Pray for them. Help them discover their gifts and potential so that if and when the time comes, they are ready to serve.

7. HOW CAN MY CHURCH HELP NEW BELIEVERS SEEK A QUIET AND GODLY LIFE?

There's an old saying that we become what we celebrate. Western churches—especially American churches—*love* to celebrate big numbers, big actions, and big personalities. This love makes us gravitate to the anomalies, especially to megachurches and culture warriors. But the chances are high that you're not leading a megachurch. As for culture warring, if you've read this book you know I am not a fan, even though I wholeheartedly affirm that Christians should be fully engaged in the public square.

So how do you encourage new believers to seek a quiet and godly life, the way 1 Thessalonians 4 commands? First, teach them that this is the expectation from Scripture. Help them to see how the Bible commends this type of lifestyle. New believers won't know that this is truly the expectation unless it's taught, so teach them. Second, celebrate the examples that exist within your church. Hold the people who model this well—people who don't engage with all the hubbub and hysterics of the day—as people worthy of emulation, encouraging new believers to follow them as they follow Christ (1 Corinthians 11:1). Third, and most importantly, live this way yourself. If this is the way God wants us to live (and it is), then we have to lead by example. Mind your own business. Don't get involved in matters that don't affect you. Don't compare your church to a one in Texas if you're in Vermont. Don't try to make a name for yourself because it's entirely possible that God has called you to be ignored. So be faithful in that. Love Jesus, love the people in your church, and love your community.

A FINAL WORD OF ENCOURAGEMENT

We're living in a strange new world, and it's getting stranger by the day. Culture is changing faster than any one human can keep up, and it's easy to become overwhelmed. And guess what? Adult new believers feel that way too. Remember, becoming a Christian is entering into a whole new culture as well. As nervous as you are about what you might see coming in the world, an adult new believer is equally uncertain about what it means to live as a Christian. They want—no, they *need*—your help.

The good news is you can help. No matter how ill-equipped you feel, no matter how unexpected their questions might be, God has put you in their lives for a reason. He has given you "everything required for life and godliness through the knowledge of him who called us by his own glory and goodness" (2 Peter 1:3). With his help, and in his power, you have everything you need to pass this on to new believers as well.

PUT IT ON A MIX TAPE

I grew up in the era of the mix tape. As a teenager, I spent hours working tirelessly on cassette tapes, and later CDs, making lists, adding songs, removing others, and moving the order around, all to share music I loved with others. Actually, it was mostly to share my inner thoughts and feelings with girls since I didn't know how to express myself well. What better way to tell the girl you're into how you feel than by presenting a tape, right?[1]

Even though tapes and CDs have more or less fallen out of favor, and I am a lot better at expressing myself, I still make the modern equivalent: playlists. I have playlists for every occasion. Some are to help me as I go through different exercises and tasks like writing, commuting to work, going for a walk, and so forth. Others are built for different holidays and life events. Occasionally I'll build one to give my kids a snapshot of me at certain stages of life.

As a storyteller and all-around nerd, I also love easter eggs. It's a treat to discover the winks and nods to fans that pop up in

---

1. This rarely works out well, just for the record.

different films, TV, songs, and even books. Not everyone notices them, but when you're in the know, you know. (Y'know?)

So why am I telling you all this, especially now that the book is done? This book is filled with easter eggs, if you know what to look for, and especially if you're a fan of pop, new-wave, punk, and alternative music. Every chapter title comes from a different song from the 1970s through the 2010s. None of these songs could be classified as Christian, and at least a couple have lyrics that run contrary even to the content of the book itself (which is actually the point in a couple of instances). In some cases they speak to the cultural ideas we all soak in every day. In other cases, they speak to a larger truth represented in the book despite themselves. Because I couldn't help myself, I made you a playlist that you can listen to on a couple of different streaming services. Listen and enjoy at aaronarmstrong.co/mixtape.

Thanks for reading (and listening)!

WORDS OF EXHORTATION FROM THE CHINESE CHURCH

"Let us learn from the witness of our Chinese brothers and sisters so that we can stand fast all the better as we face trials wherever we live."

— *Timothy Keller, from the foreword*

Visit lexhampress.com to learn more